CEO of YOU

Manage Your Career and Earnings for Guaranteed Success

Bethany A. Williams

Winning Strategies Book 5

Dedication

I dedicate this book to my readers and loyal supporters and fans.

I owe untold appreciation to my family that loves me despite my often unpredictable schedule; my two sons Brandon and Caleb, and my daughter Heather, her husband Brian and my granddaughter Madison. They are the joys of my life, supplying my life with love, caring, and limitless joy.

Continued thanks and appreciation goes to my much deserving editor, Amy Vanvleck, for her conscientious editing and for my stylist, Bobbi Schwartz, who keeps me dressed for success and looking like a star.

I'm blessed to have my parent's guidance and support, Jim and Elois Eastman, and my brother Bert Eastman. My mom and dad are loving souls that are passionate about helping the homeless. They spend hours at Carriage Town Ministries in Flint, Michigan. My father works as a teacher, and my mother helps out in a myriad of other ways. Should you ever have a USB drive that you would like to donate, or a used computer, they would love to have it there at the mission to help someone get back on their feet again. They can be found online at www.carriagetown.org. Please consider helping.

I owe great appreciation to my web designer, launch video creator and web editor, Jestin Jose. He has been an unexpected blessing in my life, bringing innovative technological advances and great ideas to my web site and book launch videos.

For each and every one that reads this book, I hope for you great success and happiness.

Bethany Williams

Table of Contents

CEO of YOU

Introduction

Your career path, jobs that you have access to, your network, and the opportunities presented to you rest entirely on your shoulders. You are responsible to manage your career path and your earnings.

This new job market and economy has brought with it monumental shifts that, translated, means that y*our role has irrevocably changed!* It hasn't always been this way. If statistics weigh true, the average worker will change jobs every 2-3 years and have more than 26 jobs in a lifetime.

Not that long ago, career paths and career management was the responsibility of your employer. It made sense for your employer to invest in their people, train them, and ensure that they were positioned properly to end up in exactly the right role to match their skillsets and capabilities.

Then everything changed.

Seemingly overnight, average job tenures declined from ten to twenty years to two to four years. Companies immediately shifted their focus to hiring the right talent, not, for the most part, growing their talent. So, what does this mean for you? It has left YOU in charge of your career and career path.

You are now responsible to manage your career and maximize your earnings. You have become the CEO of YOU. *How will you ensure that your maximum earnings are attained?* What steps and plans will you put in place to catapult your capabilities, skillsets, and brand to the top of a very competitive global pile?

CEO of YOU

Described within the pages of *CEO of YOU* are the action steps proven to create demand and profits for you. This is a do-it-yourself career management guidebook.

It is time to shift your thinking and begin thinking of yourself as a product. You own the rights to YOU. You are the CEO, chief marketing officer, chief financial officer, chief human resources officer, brand champion, asset manager, and stylist for you. You own the YOU Enterprise.

It doesn't matter if you are unemployed, or earning seven figures a year, or anywhere in between. Each one of you has a daunting task. How will you manage the assets of the YOU Enterprise?

The answers lie ahead. Stay tuned. I'm about to turn your main focus from your company to YOU.

Bethany A. Williams

Chapter 1: YOU as a Managed Asset

Focus on Your Career and Your Market Value

Your earnings over your career will add up to the largest asset that you will ever own. You may not have thought of yourself as an asset, but your earning potential is a gold mine of financial opportunity. It is as if you are sitting on a mattress of money and haven't thought about how to invest it. YOU have market value. YOU are an asset that needs to be managed to maximum potential earnings. Mismanagement can cause catastrophic financial loss.

You are the asset manager of your past, present, and future earnings. This is a concept you freely acknowledge and accept with regards to your retirement earnings and income. You know that you need to closely think through and manage those monies. You meet with advisors, calculate the time value of money and spend time managing the 1-10% of your earnings that you are contributing to a 401K or a retirement account. Now, it is time to apply that same concept to the earnings that you will collect throughout your career. Your job is to ensure that your earnings reach the highest potential as fast as possible and remain high for as long as you can maximize those earnings.

If you own a house, a car, or anything of value, then you understand the concept of market value. If your car, for example, has leather seats, those seats raise the market value of your car. YOU have market value. What is the market value of YOU? This is not about how much money you make today. Think about it as a 'blue book' value for YOU and your skillsets.

What will your skills, combined with your experience, personality and specialty characteristics yield in the market? By combining your education, experience, skillsets, unique differentiators, passions and skills, you can calculate your worth. You can come up with a rough market value for YOU. Unlike a car, your value will go up with years of experience and as you develop skills. And, much like a house, adding renovations and upgrades will increase your value. If you started a company, for example, your worth could expand exponentially.

Your value will follow a bell curve, moving upwards for most of your career. You will then hit a peak, and your earnings will begin to decline at a certain age and level of experience unless you start a business or develop a passive income stream.

Illustration1: *Earnings bell curve*

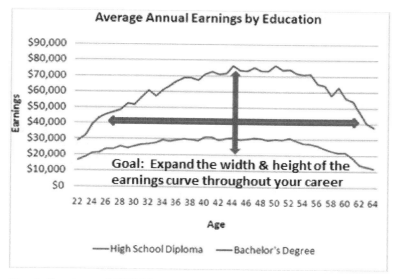

Graph Courtesy of CBS Money Watch

CEO of YOU

Key Point:
Your goal is to maximize the bell curve, working to get it higher earlier in your career, and then maintain a higher value for an extended period of years.

Your job as asset manager of your earnings is to maximize your earnings during the time period that you are on an upward spike. You have a limited amount of time to earn money before your earnings curve will begin to head downward. Often the bell curve begins to maintain at age forty, and then slowly move in a downward trend. Your goal is to maximize the bell curve, working to get it higher earlier in your career, and then maintain a higher value for an extended period of years. A small increase in the beginning of your bell curve will compound over the tenure of your earnings life. If your employer, for example, offered you a bonus rather than adding a raise to your salary early in your career, this would cause your earnings curve to rise slower over the long haul, causing a significant loss in compounded earnings. This isn't always your first thought when it comes to your salary and earnings.

It is important to identify your skills and how they are valued, especially in this global economy. Locate and review one or many of the websites that are available for you to explore. Salary.com is a great source for salary data. There are also compensation surveys that you can purchase and/or find easily on the web. It is well worth the investment of your time to determine your market worth for your job type, company size, responsibilities, and location(s).

Your market value today is your starting point. With upgrades to your education, skillsets or experience, it can change positively.

You could be more valuable than the salary you currently make reflects, but the right people that would hire you may not be aware that you exist or you are living in a geographic area where your skillsets are not in-demand. You'll learn about your personal brand, brand awareness, marketing and selling yourself, as you move through the pages of this book.

We, for the most part, march through our careers accepting the status quo. If someone advises us the value of our skills, we believe them, and accept the job they offer us with a smile. We usually don't shop around the way we do when we purchase a car and we often don't dedicate time and energy to a 'blue book' market evaluation of our earning potential. We don't even consider starting a business or researching other areas we can use our strengths.

Well, now is the time. What are your core skills worth? How do your skills compare to the market? Are you in a field that is growing or declining? What geographic areas have a demand for your skill-set? Diligently work to put a dollar value on your current market worth. Use comparative values for similar job postings and job openings. Use salary websites and surveys to take an educated guess as your worth. Put a market value down on paper.

CEO of YOU

You should spend four to six hours a year with an outplacement specialist or career coach even when you have a job. Just because you haven't been laid off or fired doesn't mean that you are maximizing your market value or taking advantage of market opportunities.

Would you ever choose your own investments for your 401K without research and reviewing the returns? Consider the magnitude of your earnings across your entire career. You're probably putting somewhere between one to ten percent of your salary into your 401K. It should get LESS planning and attention than your total market earnings throughout your career.

Are you spending an adequate amount of time or attention ensuring that you are maximizing your market value? Chances are high, very high, that you are not. The result could be a poorly managed YOU asset.

This asset cannot sit on a shelf. It will not grow without a plan. It will not become amazing by itself. You will have to manage the asset that is YOU; your active earnings and all passive revenue driven from the YOU brand.

Maybe you are thinking that you don't have passive revenue. Well, today is the day to start thinking of yourself like a business. If you can drive passive revenue from the YOU Enterprise in book sales, DVD sales, CDs, photography, or X (you name it), why wouldn't you? Why wouldn't you figure out ways to make money for you— using skills you have learned throughout your life? You may decide to put a plan in place that you don't implement for six to ten years. We will cover the potential to develop your passive revenue stream in Chapter 7: Your Financial Growth Plan. Don't rule it out without consideration. There may be gold lying in wait in a stream somewhere in your life.

A well-executed plan, exercised over time is equivalent to 'bonus money' as the years pass. It is the ultimate benefit of making your skillsets pay-off for you. So many of you have ideas and plans that have crossed your mind, yet you've never devoted even an hour of thinking about it. You take time planning for the companies you work. You work diligently; no doubt, to make sure the company you are devoted to is very profitable. What about you and your money, future, and best interests? You are procrastinating. You believe that since you will not start on the plan for 3-5 or even 7 years, why begin your plan today? You need to start your plan because without it, it will not materialize. Without the plan, it will not grow, and most probably won't ever happen.

Think of an enterprise you know and respect. Let's take Vera Wang Enterprise as an example. Although focused on fashion, she expanded to interior decorations to increase her footprint and profits. She took a skillset and expanded it to increase revenues. You should start thinking like Vera Wang.

Investing and Adding Upgrades

This is a great time to invest in YOU. Investing in yourself and adding additional skillsets to the portfolio of YOU can help you to reap better financial benefits and ensure a job when others struggle to find and keep one. It can also translate into increased life satisfaction. If you plan this well, the upgrades you add will be something related to subjects and activities that you truly enjoy and are drawn to. You can add 'fun' into your work life with a plan that incorporates education, classes, lessons, or plans in areas that you enjoy.

Kristen Kaufman writes in a Plaid for Women article on leadership, *Initiate, Invest, and Engage*:

> "I am referring to other ways of investing such as, furthering our education, enhancing our careers, joining new organizations and 'tribes' of people, soliciting outside perspectives and so on. Now is the time to 'shore up' what we individually and collectively offer to the world and our respective markets. Now is the time to evaluate our offerings, reconsider our approach, strengthen our competitive differentiations, and clarify our value propositions.
>
> Now is the time to invest – both in time and money – to ***ensure we are optimizing what we are, what we have, and what we do***. Now is the time to leverage other people and resources to help us achieve (and exceed) our goals."[4]

She does a great job of explaining the urgency in evaluating what we have to offer and reconsidering our approach.

There are numerous ways to increase your market value and invest in yourself. Here are a few ideas to consider as you move to the next step on the journey:

1) Research your industry

2) Find new trends
3) Attend online webinars
4) Read magazines and literature in your field
5) Consider online courses to advance your knowledge
6) Evaluate additional college, certifications, programs and other educational opportunities

You should know your industry and business better than anyone; and, if you don't yet find yourself in this valuable position, it is never too late to begin. Research your market. Evaluate your competition. Look at what others are doing. What's on the horizon? Map out a course of education and training that keeps your skillsets in the demand curve.

What new areas are popping up that you could take advantage of? Are their new regulations that you can read up on, or new segments of standard practice or best practices that you can become an expert on? Think about creating a niche where you take on a greater depth of knowledge than your counterparts. Are there certifications in your field you could consider obtaining? Begin to map out a 'stand out' strategy that benefits both you and your organization.

Do you know what the top paying certifications are? Based on the Global Knowledge Special Report[12], the top 5 are as follows, in order of highest pay:

- PMP: Project Management Professional
- CISSP: Certified Information Systems Security Professional
- MCSD: Microsoft Certified Solutions Developer
- MCDBA: Microsoft Certified Database Administrator
- and CCDA: Cisco Certified Design Associate.

CEO of YOU

The total list and average salaries can be found in the reference table in the back of this book. Decide if it makes sense to invest in these certification programs or others that map specifically to your field or an interest that you have.

Online webinars make education convenient in today's busy world. Setup a few Google alerts on topics that are of interest to you. Search through twitter for webinars of interest. Put them on your calendar. Take notes and learn something new. Share the knowledge you've learned with others at your company. Begin attending online webinars on the topics on a regular basis. Become an expert. Learn and grow your knowledge and skillsets.

Read magazines and literature in your field. Stay up to date on trends and new movements in your industry. Forward copies of important tidbits you find in your research to your peers and bosses. Staying up to date on the market is essential for becoming an employee with valuable market worth and staying power.

Don't stop there. Join a professional network and gain visibility within your industry. Be aware of developments in your industry and make a reputation for yourself. Work hard to get a good position within your networks. Represent yourself in the best possible way, authoring articles and engaging in work groups that can expand other's awareness of YOU.

Stanford has a Center for Professional Development. Have you ever considered going back to school? Consider taking one or two courses to activate your mind and increase your knowledge and market value. You are responsible to continue to add upgrades to YOU to make yourself worth more and increase your market value. Start with one small step.

Managing Your Trip up the Jungle Gym

If you are looking to advance into higher positions, than you will need a plan to climb the ladder. In her book *Lean In*, Sheryl Sanberg uses the analogy of maneuvering a jungle gym rather than climbing a corporate ladder. She quotes Pattie Sellers, senior editor for Fortune Magazine, who believes your career is more like a jungle gym than a ladder. A jungle gym allows you to move around in several creative ways to get where you are going (i.e., the top!). Some moves are lateral; while some are one rung up at a time. Your challenge is to forge a unique path to get you where you'd like to go.

Whatever path you decide to take, your goal is to manage your long-term vision of where you'd like to go and be prepared to find and jump on opportunities along the way.

I decided when I wrote *Brand YOU* that I would accept all calls from every recruiter that contacted me. As my profile grew and popularity ensued, this has become a daunting and almost impossible task. I began listening to opportunities, all opportunities, if only to give names of others that may make excellent candidates. I became acutely aware of the vast canvas of opportunities that exist across my regional area, the US, and an ever-broadening market that spans continents and countries.

CEO of YOU

Often we get busy in a role and we close ourselves off to other opportunities. Managing your career and lifetime earnings involves listening with an ear to the ground, always being aware of your need to stay focused on potential opportunities that could benefit your next jungle gym move.

When we accept the status quo and get comfortable in our jobs, we stop strategizing and stop playing the 'advancement game' mid-job. We tend to focus only on success in that role. When you aren't focused on being two steps toward the door because the job is providing you what you need, you settle in and accept things as they are and you miss opportunities.

Most people that I talk to who find themselves suddenly out of work fit that status-quo category. They never suspected their sudden 'exit' and are caught surprised and unprepared. You cannot afford to be caught surprised and you cannot let yourself be unprepared. Unprepared means that you are not managing your career well. Unprepared means that you are at the whim of your company and could be caught in a buy-out, leadership change, or sudden market change that leaves you with few to no options.

As the recruiting agent of YOU, your attention needs to be both focused on your current position and your next one, should you ever need a next one. Be prepared for the inevitable and ready for a surprise change in your employment. Being vigil and slightly focused on other opportunities on occasion will ensure that your interests are always protected and your future secure.

But, how do you find the time? This is the most common question posed to me. It is not about dedicating an intense amount of time to your 'watch plan.' It is about *having* a watch plan. It is about an occasional discussion and a focus. It is a thought process that dedicates *some* time to the possibility of another, better opportunity opening up elsewhere. Often it isn't just about discovering opportunities; it is about creating them.

Creating Opportunities

It is an easy and logical thought process to think about creating opportunities and constantly looking at bettering a position when we think of our spouse or our children's situation. But, when we think of ourselves, we aren't always inclined to think this way. Our natural dislike of change keeps us from focusing on it. We can't disconnect from the thought of the impact of it long enough to allow our mind to consider other options.

The best skill to develop is the ability to brainstorm options and possible alternate positions and career paths in pure brainstorming mode. You may even try to convince yourself that you are thinking up possible paths for someone you know with skills exactly like yours, not for yourself directly. Refuse to allow yourself, initially, to rule anything out because of location, title, responsibilities, etc. Develop the ability to dream up possible paths you could take and a vision of your future, no matter what part of your career you find yourself in. Do whatever it takes to begin getting YOU to think about your future and alternate career path options.

CEO of YOU

What do you envision for your career in five or ten years? Have a goal in mind for your long-term path as well as a shorter twelve- month plan. It is time to map out a plan and investigate your options. Your company isn't going to do it for you.

You probably have more potential than you've ever considered. You have probably set your goals too low and conveniently left your dreams and aspirations behind you. Closely evaluate your potential. Look at your skills, talents, and experiences as if you were looking at those of a stranger. Project 'stretch positions' and consider paths that could catapult you closer to the position that best utilizes your skills and talents. Dream up a goal for attainment. Create a dream that incorporates the position that you want to have and the desires of your heart. Write it down. Create 'first steps.' What actions would you start with to move you closer to a job that fulfills your heart's desire?

Finding Your Worth

What are you worth? It's possible, even easily foreseeable, that given the right company and the right position for you, you could be worth two or three times what you are currently making. We often undervalue ourselves. We cut ourselves short, and in doing so, we live less than amazing lives doing jobs that are less than exciting or fulfilling. We settle. We get trapped in mediocrity and we stop seeking 'the WOW factor.' I'm asking you to dream up a market value and trajectory for YOU and to dream up your WOW.

Calculate the maximum potential that you believe that you can earn. Then ask two or three of your biggest fans, "What do you believe that I am capable of achieving? What do you believe my maximum earning potential is?" You may be surprised, probably shocked, at the answers.

My first response from one of the executives that knows me well and I greatly respect was that I was worth a million dollars a year (no, it didn't come with a job offer). That was more than I'd set as my own potential. I had undervalued the possibilities. Have you undervalued your possibilities? Are you looking at your potential with an open perspective?

If you are jobless, have you considered a jungle gym approach to where you want to arrive? A job, any job, in a company that you admire is better than no job at all. Start somewhere. It is a bit like a battle with weight. Losing weight is better in small quantities than losing none at all.

Get your foot in the door. Start by accepting that 'first' role. Figure your maximum potential and then move upward and onward toward your earning potential and the position that you desire. Ask someone that interviews you to place you in a lower level position that will put your skills to work, assuming they cannot hire you for the position that you applied for because it is 'frozen.' Use your ingenuity. Strategize and plan a way to start somewhere. Companies often promote from within. Get within. Get in the door. Move it! Make it happen.

Don't count on your hiring manager to know what you should be worth. I've seen many an executive low bid on starting salary by a hiring manager that they trusted, even one that was a close friend. Know your value. Research your worth. Negotiate for your worth. I discovered when I was working at Perot Systems Corporation, that the female executives normally accepted their job offer with no negotiation, while the men would, on average, negotiate for 8-12 weeks! Who do you think received the higher pay?

CEO of YOU

Ask for what you'd like to be paid. Negotiate your worth and starting salary. Be bold.

Just two weeks ago I met a woman who has been in her current role for fifteen years. She now realizes that since she has fallen so far under market value, it has become difficult if not impossible to get a job outside of her current company. She is finding that external companies do not believe that she has the experience and qualifications that she has since she is so far under market value. You could be preventing yourself from getting a great position with great pay because you have allowed your pay to drop alarmingly below the market value that you should be making. You are doing yourself a disservice. Make it a goal to increase your worth. Can you commit to interview for roles that pay you what your market value should be? Since a low current salary can keep you from getting another role, be sure to say, "I would not leave my current role for less than X." Make X what you should be making.

> **Key Point:**
> *You could be preventing yourself from getting a great position with great pay because you have allowed your pay to drop alarmingly below the market value that you should be making.*

Focus on knowing your market value and a plan to increase your worth. It is an important first step in managing your career and furthering your income.

Chapter 2: Personal Brand Equity

Taking Stock of Your Brand Equity

It is time to take stock of your brand equity. To be known for your skillset and strengths is a valuable asset. If companies, executives and people think of you when they think of certain needs that they have in organizations, than your brand has great value. If they do not, then your brand needs work. Have you created a brand worthy of YOU? What is your brand equity worth?

Company brands have succeeded, and failed, over the years. We have watched the successes, and known little about the failures. The failures are ripped from the shelves, off into the land of obscurity and we don't hear about them, purchase them, or know of their existence.

Have you ever worn a pair of Bic disposable underwear? Me neither, and apparently neither did many others. Yet, Bic really did create disposable underwear. The thought of buying underwear from company that makes writing utensils didn't turn out to be a successful idea.

Did you serve Colgate Kitchen Entrees for dinner last night? I don't think so. Moms decided quickly that it wasn't a desirable brand for meals that they wanted to feed their family.

Do you drive a Volkswagen Thing or a DeLorean? Both not-so-popular car products were failed attempts at creating a successful brand.

I've read my share of *Cosmopolitan* magazines and they are, by many measures, one of the most popular magazines of the times. *Cosmopolitan* has 58 international editions, is published in thirty-six languages and is distributed in more than one hundred countries, making it one of the most dynamic brands on the planet. I'd say they have their magazine brand down to a science. All the more reason why it is surprising that they would choose to sell yogurt. Yes, I did say yogurt. From the time of its release, the yogurt was pulled off the shelves within eighteen months.

Every component of our lives is touched by brands and branding. We are exposed to information, packaging, and branding on a daily basis. We make decisions and choose purchases based on our knowledge and experience with brands.

As CEO of YOU, your responsibility is to create a brand that keeps you from being an obscurity. Your brand can and should be known to those in your company, and even in your industry. It is time to build brand equity. You must set a course that positively brands YOU into a KNOWN entity, places you "in demand" to start or continue to work a job that you love. You are your brand champion.

I cover the details of personal brand development in *Brand YOU*, walking you through the steps to developing a personal brand that can best announce YOU in a market wrought with stiff competition. Do you know what you want to be known for? Have you created a stellar brand? If you haven't, now is the time to layout your brand and your brand strategy. Define who you want to be known as.

Once you've identified a personal brand for yourself, you will need to regularly take stock of your brand equity and value. Who knows what you can do? Have you marketed your brand well both inside and outside of your company? Are you considered an expert in a specialty area for your company? Once you have defined your brand, and made it fabulous, it is time to take YOU to the next level.

Evaluating Your Brand

You are not your job title. You are not a business manager, architect or accountant. You are a compilation of the characteristics and skill sets that you use in your position. You are the skills and talents that, if branded well, can pay off for you in increased business opportunities and a better future for yourself. Sherry Beck Paprocki, branding expert and co-author of *The Complete Idiot's Guide to Branding Yourself*, says "If you don't brand yourself, Google is going to do it for you!"

Think slick. Think of well-polished ideas. Do you describe yourself in the best light possible? Think of yourself as a new product that Sony or Apple has just developed. How would you describe and package the product to be appealing and purchasable? What would make you want to buy it? Why would a company pay for your services? What do you have to offer? Does your brand meet this criteria? Do you stand out? If not, what would it take to stand out?

Regularly research some of your competition. Think of people in your industry whom you consider to have similar skills and experience to yours. Research them. Look up their bios. Explore their experience and employment history on LinkedIn. Compare your brand to theirs.

Put on the 'thinking cap' of CEO. What would motivate a CEO to hire you as opposed to someone else? This is a new economy. Critical thinking is necessary. Critical personal brand valuation is a requirement. You will not be able to continue to grow and thrive unless you retool and rethink. It is time to get going. Brand development is a necessity of the new economy and a well-developed brand can and will pay off handsomely.

Evaluate your LinkedIn profile. Your LinkedIn profile is more than an online resume. It is an online billboard that advertises YOU. It is a reflection of your brand. It should show the return on investment that companies have benefited from having YOU on their payroll. It should be a results-oriented view of YOU. The reader should be excited about what YOU could do for his/her company. It is your brand statement clearly defined and for all to see.

When you look at information about others, what JUMPS out at you? What amazes you? Your brand and profile should AMAZE others. It is a competitive landscape. SPEND SOME TIME ON evaluating your brand and refining it. Keep refining it until it jumps off the page. Find profiles that you like and focus on key words that got your attention. Use them in your description. Your brand should be clearly defined and spelled out in your LinkedIn profile.

Creating & Developing Your Brand Plan

You should have a brand plan. As CEO and Chief Marketing Officer of YOU, you are responsible to create your brand, develop it and know the interval with which you will review your brand. You are the creator of invigorating new ideas that catapult your brand further than the others in the market and ensure success for you in whatever field you have chosen. Your responsibility is to create a brand that drives demand even in markets that are competitive. You need to drive demand toward the YOU brand. Higher demand equals higher pay, continued job success, and increased opportunities. What can you do to create a unique brand that will bring others to seek your services? What can you do to put YOU in demand?

I recently met a caricaturist in Orlando Florida. He is in a very competitive market. He determined over a year ago that he needed to go digital to enhance his brand and further his business opportunities. He bought a digital tablet, and he uses it to create the cartoons. He then prints the digitally created images and is able to send digital copies to patrons that have received his services.

Since Orlando is a hub of convention activity, he has

ensured continued business success and set his business apart from others in the market. His business card also highlights his brand. He has created an innovative, creative, differentiating brand that has ensured that he is working when others are not.

Left: e-Tablet used by caricaturist Rafael Diez in Orlando

Below: Cartoon of Bethany created by Rafael

Right: Caricaturist's Business Card

CEO of YOU

Every market niche has examples that you can find of true innovation and brands that jump out at you. Real estate has been a tough market. The demand has not kept up with the supply. It has left many people struggling to find other jobs to supplement their waning income. In Texas, in the Dallas/Fort Worth area, a group of realtors have built a distinct brand, the Mike Mazyck Group, found on the web at mikesrealtygroup.com. Their slogan is 'the way real estate should be.' Mike Mazyck and group have built an amazing brand, a distinct message and market by grabbing up listings that no one else could sell and building a name for themselves. Their unique and effective marketing programs have put them on the map. They stand out.

They are memorable and different. They also offer a moving van, available free to those that use their service, branded clearly as the Mazyck Group. It's brilliant. In a market when there are too many real estate agents, Mike and team have positioned themselves to get the calls. They have done what many wish to do; they have created a sellable brand that occupies a distinct place in the minds of others.

They have created a fully rounded-out brand strategy with an amazing, easy-to-search web site, and a consistent ability to 'do' what they say they will do. The people they serve speak well of them. They have succeeded where many have failed. Powerful branding makes for a strong brand experience. They have created an amazing brand, created the service and experience to support it, and marketed that brand to their target audience in defined areas.

Competitive market spaces necessitate exciting and innovative brands. Michael Williams is the CEO and owner of PrinterSmart, found on the web at printersmart.com. He is in a competitive market space, delivering print services, ink and toner cartridges, printers, and mobile phone repair both locally and to a national marketplace. Even though he is a small business owner, he has spent the time to develop his brand.

He developed a logo, a catch phrase, and even a mascot to stand out in his field.

*Printer*Smart

"We will always take great care of you!";

Printer Supplies | Equipment | Parts & Repairs | Print & Copy Services | Over 75 National Distribution Centers

*Printer*Smart uses Professor *Printer*Smart in advertisements, prints him on giveaways, and uses him to reinforce his brand. Williams has developed a big company brand to further the growth of his business. He has created a brand that stands out and pulls patrons into his business, and he has captured business from large national corporations.

Brand development is important. It can catapult your personal brand above the others. Knowing that it draws customers into places of business, think about creating messages, images, and logos for YOU to stand out and help people to remember YOU.

Your brand has to stand out. It needs to differentiate you in a sea of people. Imagine what you would do if you were the Chief Marketing Officer for *NIKE*. You would have to come up with a brand plan that would get people to buy *NIKE* over any of the other brands on the market. You would want people to think *NIKE* instead of Adidas or Reebok, Under Armour or any other.

In this same instance, you are the Chief Marketing Officer of YOU. You have to come up with a brand plan that will get people to think of YOU instead of Frank or Susan, Olivia or Fred. YOU have to have a superior brand and a brand plan that will differentiate your brand from all the others. Even if you are successfully working in a company and a position that you love today, you still need to focus on a brand plan that will get you to stand apart from all others. In this economy, everyone needs a brand plan because we are all standing on unstable ground.

When I was writing *Brand YOU*, I worked with a few key executives to identify their brand and move it to the next level. One of those executives was Dr. Harry Greenspun. Within two years, Harry catapulted from anonymity to having his own Wikipedia.

When you Google Harry, this is what you find:

He has selected both the image, and the words that he wants associated with his brand, and he continues to ensure that his brand is consistent wherever it appears. In 2010, *Modern Healthcare* magazine named Dr. Greenspun one of the "50 Most Powerful Physician Executives in Healthcare."[6]

He successfully stands out from the pack of physicians. In a large national space, he has created a unique, distinctive brand that makes him different from all others.

What personal brands have you admired? Have you seen fabulous brands that made you stop and take notice? I've seen numerous examples of branding success.

Jim Champy is another great example of branding success. He built a successful career in management consulting, and published a book in the 90s titled, *Re-engineering the Corporation*. It was a publishing success, selling millions of copies in more than thirty languages and considered one of the best business books of the 90s.

Jim has taken his success and created a brand around the re-engineering phenomena.

JIM CHAMPY

Innovation | Insight | Strategy

His logo is simple; the words *Innovation, Insight, and Strategy* follow his name. He is re-engineering. He has created several other books. OutSmart was one of my favorites. His website JimChampy.com reinforces his brand. He is a shining example of branding success.

LinkedIn Singapore has created a list of the most-viewed profiles in Singapore. With over a million people on LinkedIn in Singapore, what do you think it takes to stand out? Seven profiles stand out for technology. Seven! Seven stand out in a sea of a million. These power profiles have one thing in common: they have created magnificent brands and images. None of their photos were shot from their cell phone in the driver's seat of their car. They look professional. Their summaries are well written.

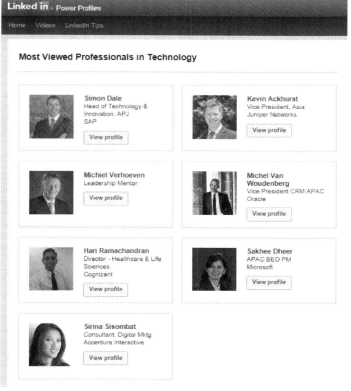

CEO of YOU

LinkedIn sent out notices on their top-viewed profiles. They recognized their members that had reached the top one , five , and ten percent. When a LinkedIn representative was asked what the benefit was of being in the top percentile, they replied: "The practical upside to being the top one or five percent is that we believe the more engaged you are on LinkedIn, the better you will be in the job that you currently have, and the better connected when you are seeking a new job."

I agree with their assessment. You are responsible to increase awareness of your brand. It will help you both within your organization and if and when you decide to look for work. Like ad placements, the more often the ad is seen, the higher the impressions and therefore, the higher the value created.

How's this for a summary? " Lilach is a business owner, social media consultant, internet mentor and founder of Socialable.co.uk. Listed in *Forbes* for the Top 20 Women Social Media Power Influencers, she is one of the most dynamic personalities in the social media market. She actively leverages ethical online marketing for her clients and her own advantage." Lilach Bullock knocks it out of the park with this summary. You can tell from the picture she uses that she is listed by Forbes for the Top 20 Women. She enforces her brand with the images and words that she uses. Are you getting inspired yet?

Now does it all make sense? Do you understand the importance of creating a brand and a brand plan to make you sensational? Have you thought of brand images, catch phrases and words that you could use that stand for you?

Start by creating a brand plan that includes the following:

- **Define your brand:** What do you want to be known for?
- **Create a distinct brand for YOU or your business that includes:**
  - Your message
  - Your biography
  - Your key brand elements
    - These must stand out
    - These need to create demand for your services
- **Market/Advertise your brand**
- **Use social media to advance your brand**

CEO of YOU

Details on building your personal brand and the creation of your brand plan can be found in my book, *Brand YOU*. This detailed step-by-step guide takes you through an intricate path to develop a personal brand plan that will help you stand apart from all others.

In order to market yourself in a distinctive way, think of ways not used by others to market and sell them. Think about how you could create and strengthen a brand through a strong consistency of service and messaging. You will need to set a level of expectations that you will then consistently fulfill. Think outside the box. Create a stellar brand that can then be messaged and marketed out to your audience.

We will walk through innovative marketing ideas, great messaging, creating spectacular resumes and info-graphics in Chapter 5: Marketing YOU.

Chapter 3: A Personal Board of Directors for YOU- yes YOU!

The Critical Need to Build Your Own Personal Board of Directors

Companies understand the importance of getting it right. Show me a successful company with amazing leaders and I'll show you a smart, savvy Board of Directors (BOD) that keeps the company on track.

So, why would companies pay leaders and CEOs high salaries, hire informed, talented, and bright leadership, yet still feel the need to have talented and visionary Board of Directors? To make sure that all bases are covered, they recruit and maintain a talented and diverse Board of Directors. They take every action possible to be positive that they are going down the right path and not missing any unidentified threats or opportunities.

Companies depend on a talented Board of Directors to ensure continued and predictable success. This security blanket ensures that their investors' interests are well protected and great strategy and decisions are continually made. They make sure to secure valuable investments.

What you earn throughout your career is a valuable investment. Your earnings are a large component of the key to your financial success and viability over time. Early in my career I decided that I couldn't afford missed opportunities or unidentified threats to my income source, my investment in myself. Therefore, I established a personal Board of Directors. I put this cross-industry team together to guide my career choices and my career path.

Imagine if all your career decisions were reviewed by a talented Board of Directors that you had hand-selected to manage your career. It's brilliant. It makes perfect sense. They may see something that you do not see.

There isn't a significant time commitment on their part. You are identifying three to five people that would be willing to take a couple calls from you a year to guide your career path and decisions. They are experts with necessary skillsets on the market and leadership. This isn't about a major time commitment; but about tapping into their knowledge and networks to help advance your career and earnings. A few minutes of their time will be immensely valuable to you.

This board will advise you on your career path, on companies that may make sense for you to pursue and will weigh in on job offers and positions that you are evaluating. They can advise you if the compensation package that you've been offered is market value, fair, and equitable. This priceless information will help guide your path and ensure that no opportunities or threats are missed.

They may mention that the rumors in the market indicate company instability or executive dissention in a company for whom you currently work, or are considering working. Their valuable feedback and insight will help you to make the best career decisions and help you to manage the valuable assets of your CAREER and your EARNINGS. You could get early warning signals of a buy-out or reduction in force at your current employer.

Key Point:
Your career decisions can be reviewed by a talented
Board of Directors that you have hand selected to
manage your career. It's brilliant. It makes perfect
sense. They may see something that you do not see.

My personal Board of Directors is comprised of a group of
executives that I have met and come to respect throughout
the years. They are smart, savvy, business executives in a
variety of industries. One of my personal board members
is in healthcare, the vertical that I've devoted all of my
career. A cross-functional team representing varying
verticals and positions in industry is best to get the most
variability from their viewpoints and guidance. Three, four
or five of the same opinions isn't as helpful as if five
people are weighing in that have varying viewpoints that
can help you to see all components of the picture. Each of
their views will provide you a valuable puzzle piece in
evaluating your opportunities and threats.

This group can act as consultants in times of need, advising
on political situations that you find yourself in at your
current job and critical 'stay/go' decisions that arise during
the course of any position. They can encourage financial
incentives and guide you on options and packages. They
should truly have your best interests in mind.

Sometimes we lean on our bosses and mentors within our
companies. Unfortunately, oftentimes these mentors do not
have our best interests in mind. Sometimes their direct
need to succeed at work overrules your best interest. This
Board of Directors should not include anyone that works at
your company. This board will consist of neutral third
parties that can weigh in honestly and keep your best

interests in mind. Your company contacts can be mentors for you without necessitating that they serve on your board.

My Board has saved me time and time again from making wrong turns in my career. Their keen leadership and decisive abilities have helped me to make the best decisions, the best career moves, and have prevented me from making emotionally charged, not thought-out judgments. They keep me on the right track in my career, just as a Board of Directors does for its company. Employing this same strategy, my interests are protected and I'm managing my career smartly.

The unintended benefit to this BOD is that they know you and your skillsets, your interests and your desired career path. They become career advocates for you, suggesting you for positions that they hear about and thinking of you for opportunities at their companies and their peer's companies. Even if I don't have a career question, I call these individuals one to two times a year to stay in touch.

They don't know that I think of them as my personal Board of Directors. They know I see them as advisors, and occasional mentors. I don't demand much of their time. And, they don't have it to give.

How to Create Your own B.O.D.

So, how do you go about creating a personal Board of Directors (BOD)? Let's start with the makeup of the Board.

Your BOD should be cross–industry, representing varying interests and knowledge bases. It will be made up of executives that you've become acquainted with throughout the years and have a mutual, professional respect. If you are early in your career, a favorite college professional, family friend, or mentor could be your first Board member.

My BOD is comprised of:
- Healthcare executive: a CFO for a large health system
- Recruiting executive: recruiter for C suite positions
- Software executive: senior executive at Microsoft
- Consulting partner: ex-software CEO now a partner in one of big five accounting firms
- Professional Speaker & Author: international speaker and author

As you can see, my BOD represents a financial expert, an expert on finding jobs, a business leader, an ex-CEO for big-picture thinking, and a speaker and author since I've added speaking and writing into my career plan. My BOD was carefully selected based on my interests, my relationships, and the respect that I have for these leaders. Their views are quite different and their knowledge and experiences vary greatly.

You are working to seat a diverse BOD as well. You want someone with a financial mind, someone with a CEO mindset, someone with a marketing angle, and someone with a grand economic view.

Key Point:
Your Personal Board of Directors become career advocates for you, suggesting you for positions that they hear about and thinking of you for opportunities at their companies and their peer's companies.

Select candidates that have a view of the market. You need some big-picture thinkers. Consider fields like real estate and recruiting because they see economic changes before other fields.

Ask this group to support you by saying:

> "If I call you once or twice a year, would you be willing to give me career advice and feedback? I respect your opinion and need help in managing my career and my options.
>
> I commit to not take up more than fifteen minutes each time I contact you. It isn't about a lengthy discussion; it is about getting your input at valuable times during my career journey when I need your input the most. Would you consider doing this for me? I'd really value your feedback and input."

If they say 'yes,' then you have your first Board member. Slowly build to a team. Stay in touch with them once or twice annually, beginning to build the relationship even if you have no pending decisions or career advice to ask of them.

I reach out to my personal BOD when I have a job offer that I'm considering. They weigh in. They give me candid advice. I have chosen to follow their advice, always. You will have to decide what career choices you will make based on their counsel. Truly, if you don't trust their judgment enough to make career decisions based on their input, than you haven't built the right Board. You should trust their input and judgments. Their agreed-upon goal is to help you manage your career, and help you to get the maximum value from the years that you have to dedicate to work.

Like any traditional BOD, people will move away, retire, change jobs, die, etc., and you will need to find replacement Board members as the years wear on.

Continue to focus on keeping an active personal Board of Directors and your career will flourish. Once you have them in place, it will surprise you that you ever managed without this valuable career resource and tool. It has been one of the secrets to my success and countless others with whom I have shared the information. There is no down side to this arrangement. You and your Board members benefit from the relationships formed and the knowledge gained.

Chapter 4: Your Annual Report

What have you done for your company lately?

Jobs are becoming increasingly more competitive. To compete at the top of your game, you will need easy access to your accomplishments throughout the years.

Most of us are focused on the next thing, not the last one. We lose track of our accomplishments and forge ahead, getting caught with little to talk about if/when we need to look at new opportunities. The past becomes a distant memory.

I review hundreds of resumes and LinkedIn profiles and began doing this as a guest writer for workbloom.com. I found myself often bored to tears at the LinkedIn pages and resumes that I reviewed. A good marketer or publicist could tell you what is really impressive about your history at work.

So, you are hereby sentenced to reading 350 profiles before you write or edit yours.

From them, you will see that your resume, LinkedIn profile and work summaries don't, for the most part, stand out from all others. Most don't, they aren't impressive.

You can't afford not to jump off the page! Are you jumping off the page? Evaluate yourself.

I once worked with a woman for more than four years, and never knew about a significant market award that she had received. I didn't discover it when I was helping her look for work. I had to drag it out of her after intensive interview sessions.

What makes you different than the hundreds of others out there? You have to find the answers.

Start Annualizing

The easiest way to begin remembering your successes and build upon them is to document your accomplishments annually. You need to create an annual report for YOU. Small business owners don't get this either, even in a small business you need an annual report.

You can easily start this exercise by keeping a folder on your computer or even a physical folder in a drawer. Throw in things that happen during the year that you consider accomplishments that are worth remembering. This will help you when the time comes to create your annual report.

Think about it like a tax folder. You keep it all year, throwing in receipts and pertinent information so that at 'tax time' you know how to complete your paperwork. Do the same with your accomplishments.

What were your accomplishments? It is worthwhile to put a lot of effort into the record of your successes and lessons learned. If you have very little to write about, then resolve to change that in the next year. Did you contribute to a project that is jettisoning your company forward? If not, why not do that in the next year? This annual review is your chance to document your return on investment, significant accomplishments, and ask yourself if you are really set on making a difference at your place of employment. This also is an opportunity to determine if you are not, so you can start.

If you are a busy executive, you can hire this done. Scribble down your accomplishments and hire someone to write the text explaining your accomplishments, add images, graphs, and additional content to your Word document that showcases your work to create an amazing annual report. (Yes, this is necessary in our new economy. Don't fight it.)

Start now to create a unique brand, market, and image for you even before you think it is mandatory. This will increase your demand, improve your value and ultimately create new opportunities. Stop dragging your feet. Instead of focusing on the dozen reasons why you can't do this – or think you can't do this – just think of one reason why you can.

Key Point:
This annual review is your chance to document your return on investment, significant accomplishments, and ask yourself if you are really set on making a difference at your place of employment.

Once a year, sit down and document on paper a highlight of your accomplishments. As an example, you can cover the following topics:

- **Major accomplishments**: list all major accomplishments and both their market and financial impact on the organization.

- **Return on investments**: what significant financial returns has your company seen because of your efforts?
- **New areas of interest/knowledge**: document new knowledge areas. Have you become an expert on an area that will help your company and potentially other companies as well?
- **Named expert status:** were you counted on for an article or industry publication? Did you write an article for a newsletter or speak at a conference?
- **Industry awards:** list any industry awards or recognition.
- **New responsibilities:** list new responsibilities that you've taken on, major initiatives you've undergone, etc.

This is time for a thorough review of YOU. This annual report, when combined with all the others that you will create annually will give you a summary of your accomplishments through the years. You will see where you've worked, your most significant accomplishments, and the impact that you've had on your place of employment. You will keep these annual reports, digitized, with bound and well-prepared copies, like marketing glossies, for when you need to toot your horn.

Keep digital copies backed up on your personal computer or a network share drive under your personal email address. You can use Box.com or Dropbox.com for easy storage of this important information. You can easily peruse them and use past accomplishments in future job interviews and resumes.

CEO of YOU

The purpose of this annual report is to keep an ongoing record of your contributions over time. As your brand manager, you can shape and mold the message about who you are and where you are going based on these annual reports. It will also help you, in this world of ever-changing people, to review with CEOs/bosses where you have come from and where you are going.

I have been amazed in my own career how often my CEOs/bosses have changed. It is difficult with each change to meld into a new stroke and reorient yourself to a new CEO/boss with new goals and new ideas. It is your responsibility to bring yours to the forefront; not only to help them succeed in their new role, but also to ensure that you have adequately informed them of your past contributions. As CEO of YOU, this is your responsibility.

Career death is made up of mediocre successes. You may not believe this now, but you learn infinitely more from a huge failure than you ever do from a so-so success. Coming out of a significant failure causes you to re-think. It helps you orient yourself to doing it much better next time. You don't have to experience the big failure to accomplish the same motivation. Commit to making a difference. Once you convince yourself you can, you will. It is as easy as that. This annual report is the first step to begin to advertise your success. We will cover more on advertising YOU in the next chapter.

This is not the time to downplay your success. Use power words in your write up. You didn't just 'contribute to the successful launch of'; you 'organized and led the successful launch of.' Be sure to be truthful, but also to emphasize what part you played. Use action verbs. Use more than one verb to describe the accomplishment. Sometimes our nature causes us want to humbly deny our participation or, worse, minimize it. However, we are competing for positions and PAY with others who may not 'humbly deny' their participation. Do not let others seem more qualified and successful in their initiatives than you are. Give yourself credit. This is the time to lay humbleness aside. Recognize your contribution. Write it down. Work to spread your message across the company. Create the best annual report that you've ever read.

Tie it off with a Bow

Think 'super gloss.' Visualize quotes and highlighted sections. It should have pizazz. You are advertising the annual contributions of YOU. What better way could you spend your time than documenting your accomplishments in an annual document that you will have to keep, to share, and to use as you seek opportunities in the future?

Most reviews lack oomph. They don't possess any WOW. They don't 'sell' the reader on YOU. I'm guilty of the same. Review time comes and it is another write up, another paltry attempt to summarize accomplishments in the last year. Use visuals. Think about telling a story. Make it a term paper assignment, creating ten to twenty pages of super gloss.

If you are a consultant, consider posting these summaries to your web site. Strip out customer names. Describe the project you or your company has worked on. Show results. Graph it. Sell readers on the amazing achievements you've accomplished in the last year.

CEO of YOU

Commit to being amazing. Let your brand shine through in an annual report of your accomplishments. Components of this report will be used to market you and your capabilities. This is a record of your tout-able successes.

If you've never done one in the past, first attempt a career summary report. Work on highlighting accomplishments up to this point in your career. It often takes me two to three years of knowing someone before I truly know their career accomplishments. Cut to the chase, put it on paper, put it in a word document. Add gloss. Make a PowerPoint presentation and add it via SideShare to your LinkedIn profile. Spread the word. Don't be shy. The *Nike* Marketing Manager isn't shy about how fantastic she/he thinks *Nike* is, and apparently, she/he has won that battle since we all pay thrice times as much money for something with the swoosh on it. Add your swish. Make an effort to triple markup your worth. Why not?

It is time to take it up a notch. Begin to document your accomplishments in an annual report and make it amazing. Now, let's think about Marketing YOU and take YOU a notch above *just* an annual report.

Chapter 5: Marketing YOU

You are your own enterprise. You are responsible for advertising and tracking of you/yourself as a product. Think of yourself as a corporation. You own all rights and advertising permissions for YOU. Your digital image, any articles that you've written, any speeches you've spoken, all combine to create a brand and image that markets YOU to the world.

If you create a good, sellable brand for yourself, you will be paid well. The more your brand is worth, and the more distinct and individual you can make it, the easier it will be to stay employed, create earnings opportunities, and find increased value for YOU. The best brands pull opportunities in because people know what opportunities to bring you based on your individual talents and passions.

This thinking should begin early on in your career since decisions you make early will continue to follow you throughout your career; however, it is never too late if you haven't started.

If you truly owned a product to sell, you would create a marketing plan for that product. You would envision where you want that product to go. This is no different. You need a marketing plan for you. You need to envision where you want to take the YOU Enterprise.

> **Key Point:**
> *The more your brand is worth, and the more distinct and individual you can make it, the easier it will be to stay employed, create earnings opportunities, and find increased value for YOU.*

CEO of YOU

Spend a few minutes looking up content that already exists about you. Print out everything that you find. Look it over. Consider hiring someone to evaluate your brand. What message are you sending out? Did you know that even the connections that you have on LinkedIn and the friends you have on Facebook create part of your brand? Even the descriptions people find of you when they Google you all combine to create your brand message. "You are who you choose to befriend," says Drake Baer, writer for *Fast Company* in an article about LinkedIn (April 2013).

Categorize your message ranking into one of these four categories:

- o 1: What content? I didn't find anything on myself anywhere. Grade yourself a D.
- o 2: I found some content, but it isn't very impressive. Grade yourself a C.
- o 3: I found several pieces of content that contain positive brand messages about me. Grade yourself a B.
- o 4: There is an impressive amount of content about me. It is well written, messaged, and reflects perfectly on the brand and image that I want to project. This is an A, but you can always do better; there is always A+.

When you are the Chief Marketing Officer of a company, you look at what is being said of your products and services. You study the content. It is imperative to know how the customers view your products and services. It is just as important to know how your industry views you. Not only do you need to know, but you must alter the image and brand to reflect who you really are, who you want to be known as, and include your distinct strengths and core competencies.

Marketing YOU Ideas & Examples

Before you sign off and think I'm crazy, hang on for a moment. Marketing YOU can be easy. It is about making a plan and stepping through your plan one step at a time. It can be easier than you think. You could decide to have lunch with someone in the industry that you respect, someone with a great network. You bring him/her up to date on your recent accomplishments. You just marketed yourself. It can be that easy. You can also come up with ideas that take more foresight and planning.

Here is a short list of marketing ideas to get you thinking:

- **Verbal Updates**: each time you've update someone on your accomplishments, you are marketing yourself and your capabilities.

  Sometimes this happens naturally. We run into someone that we didn't intend on running into and we are able to quickly catch up. Other times, we have to schedule time with people that we'd like to check in on, but don't occasionally run into them anymore.

  Make a concerted effort to keep a short list of professionals that you'd like to keep updated on your career and projects.

CEO of YOU

- **LinkedIn Status**: written well, a LinkedIn status updates others on something noteworthy in your career.

  Posting links to articles also updates others on the areas that you focus most of your attention. Your digital activities are branding you and sending a message to your contacts.

- **Written articles and blogs**: becoming an expert in a niche or specialty area and writing or blogging about that area will distinguish your skills from those of others. If you don't have an area that you specialize in, it is never too late to start. Start with an area that interests you.

- **Your own domain, www.YOU.com**: you can buy your own domain, allowing you to market and publicize information about YOU.

  You control the message and the content. You could use it to advertise the company you work for, or the type of work that you do. You could leave it sit unoccupied until you figure out exactly how you want to position yourself.

  In the book, *Brand YOU*, I address ways to figure out a distinct brand that can differentiate your skills from your competitors. Realize that you are competing for jobs, positions, raises, and even bonuses.

- **A fantastic resume and LinkedIn profile**: as chief marketing officer of YOU, it is imperative that you create a top-notch representation of you on both your resume and your LinkedIn profile. Both are ways to market YOU and your skillsets.

You should summarize what you do well in your LinkedIn profile. LinkedIn is a free billboard to advertise YOU and your distinct capabilities. What can you say that delineates YOUR capabilities from someone else that has similar skillsets to yours?

Surf around LinkedIn for summaries that grab your attention. Begin to summarize YOUR skillsets in a unique and differentiated way. Make your billboard shine.

- **Your network and connections**: people are your best asset. Keeping a select few updated on your career, your progress, and what you've been up to. Some of you are terrible at this, so dust off this skill and give it a workout. It will pay off for you. We will cover more of this in Chapter 10.

- **A portfolio**: if you are in marketing, sales, strategy, leadership, and other related areas, create a portfolio of your work. Include color printouts of key experiences, status reports, budgeting reports, pictures, etc. Imagine that you are a painter and you are looking for work. What evidence can you put in the portfolio to showcase YOU? Think like a marketing officer.

CEO of YOU

- **A book:** some of you might consider writing a book. Do you have experiences you'd like to share? Do you have a story to tell? Do you have a desire to create a 'How To' workbook or a guidebook? Don't wait for someone to give you permission. If a book is the best way to market yourself, than start writing.

- **An outright advertisement:** in some industries and areas, there is nothing wrong with buying ad space. Be innovative. Be original. Advertise YOU and your capabilities if it makes sense. Be bold and evaluate if it makes sense to advertise your brand.

  Just like the Mike Mazyck Group–the bold real estate agent that we discussed in Chapter 2 that advertised that he would buy your house if he couldn't sell it for you–you can advertise YOU. He chose to advertise his promise. He put his picture on the side of his car. He was bold. You can choose to do something similar if it makes sense in your industry/area, or even if it doesn't, maybe you should start a new trend.

  What would it take for you to stand out from the crowd? Figure it out. Be creative and bold as you look at opportunities to market yourself.

- **Speaking at an event:** volunteer to speak at an event about the areas on which you focus. You can start regionally and move up to national appearances.

Sometimes we recognize a goal that we want to achieve and, it is so far from where we currently are that we cannot imagine the path to get there. Start with small steps, identified and documented and then move toward those goals. I have documented a 'get it done' plan for goals in my book *Live Your Dreams*. Don't let your fears and angst keep you from starting the journey.

Document your progress. Slowly the tide will turn. Keep a journal or list of the events that you speak at. At some point, it will be prudent to add a list of events and topics that you've spoken on to your resume. This is hard to conjure up after a couple years if you didn't start documenting it from day one. Begin with the end in mind. If you know that you want to expand your brand and market yourself in this way, keep a list of the events where you speak, and slowly build.

Collateral

Every good product and company have stand out collateral materials. You read the brochures and are amazed as how well-worded it is. You can easily see the product or services benefit and the reason that you would want to purchase it. It has pictures, examples, and a compelling story. You read it and you are sold.

What does your collateral material look like? Do you have a bio that jumps off the page? Is your resume impressive? Have you developed both a personal and a business motto? Well, now is the time to develop materials that support the development of YOU as a managed product. You own how you are reflected and appear. If your company has put out a bio for you, you should review it and makes sure that it accurately reflects YOU and how YOU want to be represented. You should hire a writer to review it. You own how you are reflected and advertised. It reflects on you. It represents your brand.

Begin to build a list of collateral. Here is a sampling of possible collateral you may need to develop for the YOU Enterprise:

- Biography
- Resume
- Motto
    - Personal
    - Business
- Logo
- Press
    - Copies of any articles that you've written
    - Copies of any articles you've been quoted in
- LinkedIn Profile
    - Your skill summary
    - Your headline
    - Your references
    - Your well-described ROI
- Newsletters
- Consider purchasing your own domain
- Professional Photo- a must in today's digital world
- A bank of stories that define you
    - A 'why hire me' or 'why hire my company' story
    - A 'building trust' story
    - A company story of your best return on investment or project

Since your LinkedIn Profile can be viewed online as well as saved as a PDF, you will need to think of it as a piece of your collateral bundle as well. Go to your LinkedIn profile and save a PDF copy so that you can critique it and see how it displays in this format.

Gather copies of each of the components of your marketing materials. Develop those that you are missing. This is a reflection of how you look to the world. This is the way that YOU are reflected today. Does it accurately reflect the brand that you want to advertise? If it doesn't, recreate the components of your collateral with an eye to your brand and the key messaging that best represents YOU.

Add some gloss. Often we have the same format and look and feel of these for years. Is there a new format that would be more fresh and more unique? Later in this chapter we'll review some amazing ideas to get you thinking about new formats and visual design that might get the attention of the person, company, or CEO that you'd like to hire/notice you.

You can create newsletters about YOU. You can update your network. Think of it as the next-generation 'Christmas letter.' Think out of the box. Your job as Chief Marketing Officer of YOU is to be more creative and more unique than your competition and, literally, the other people on the planet whom you consider yourself in potential competition with for jobs, projects, and mindshare. The competition is stiff. There are more people competing for the jobs you want than ever before. Think about making the YOU product stand out in a very large, global crowd.

CEO of YOU

Your Own Website/Domain: YOU.com

More than half of all recruiters, or roughly 56 percent, are more impressed by a candidate's personal website than any other personal branding tool, according to a recent study. Yet, there is still a large amount of job seekers and employees that have not begun the development of their own website.

Purchase an internet location, a domain, that you can brand specifically for YOU. Determine the look and feel of the website, as well as explore potential names for the site. The proliferation of the web has made owning your own web site quite economical. You can buy a website that is role specific, for example www.CaliforniaAccountingGuy.com for eleven US dollars a year or www.LondonCPA.com for only a few euros a year, or one that is specific to your name; for example, www.BethanyAWilliams.com.

You don't have to possess technical skills to buy a domain. In most countries, owning a website tailored specifically for you is quite economical. They average ten to twenty US dollars a year.

So, how would you go about having your own website?

Step One:
Buy the domain and figure out the name of your website. There are several options for each country, listed here is information for the US and the UK; 1and1.co.uk, GoDaddy.com, MyDomains.com, and NamesDirect.com, are just a few of your numerous options.

Any one of these will work perfectly fine. Each service gives you an opportunity to discover naming options that are available. It is possible that the name that you'd like to buy may not be available. Begin typing possible naming conventions and see what is available to choose from. Select a name and buy the domain for a one, two, or three-year term. You don't want to wait if you see a name that you like. Grab it up before it is no longer available.

Step Two:
Now that you own the domain, you can either create a web site or hire someone to create one for you. This step doesn't need to take place the instant that you purchase your new web address. However, when you are ready, domains come with easy tools that you can use to create your own site or you can easily hire someone to do it for you.

Gone are the days that you must understand coding languages and detailed technical knowledge to use the tools provided. You might consider giving it a try. You may find that it is not as hard as you had thought it would be.

If you'd rather hire someone to create one for you, there are numerous options from teenagers that create them at home to reputable companies that can create sites for you. You have the option for US- or UK-based resources, or even hiring resources overseas. I have often used www.GetFriday.com resources to develop my web sites. They provide a cost-efficient way to create a well-constructed layout for a very reasonable price. You determine how much you want to spend to begin building your brand. You may discover that your teenager can design it for you. My son Brandon has been designing websites since before he was a teenager.

Currently Jestin Jose--a brilliant web designer that lives in India and used to be my personal assistant--designs and updates my website. Be creative. Find an excellent resource that can help you advertise and market YOU.

The finished product should reflect YOU. It should be about you, your capabilities, your aspirations, and specifics about what makes you unique. It should reflect the brand that you are developing. It should incorporate the messages that make you unique and different from the sea of others out in the market. You can consistently revamp and update the site as you progress in your career and successes. The beginning one that you develop should be just that, a launching pad for your trajectory. This is a great start on your journey to market YOU.

The Best Resume on the Planet

How do you stand out in a sea of paperwork? Many of the searches have gone online and are facilitated with keyword searches. Your resumes are now 'found' or 'not found' based on search engine words that are located on your resume.

It would be difficult to paint a picture that would accurately describe the number of resumes that have crossed my desk over the past twenty years as a hiring manager. Imagine a paper mill loaded with piles of paper and I can attest to the feeling that it could represent the number of resumes that sit on any executive's desk on any given day.

Consider the jobs and companies that you are interested in, and think about the words that a recruiter or executive would search. Think about it. Plan for it. Create a resume that covers the optimal words to be searched. Make your resume downloadable on the new website that you created for YOU.

Create two defined stories of YOU, one that represents why someone would hire you and one that is a building trust story. Learn to share and communicate these YOU stories. These stories will become assets in the YOU Enterprise. You will 'bank' these stories and use them to build your brand. Companies do this. You can see samples by typing 'Youtube success stories' in the searchbar on google.

If you are a seasoned executive, or simply don't want to make one yourself, hire someone to create an amazing reflection of your years of work. Think of a stellar way to represent what you've done or simply hire a very creative person to put it into a visual display. Why don't you consider creating an info-graphic resume?

I've attached a few samples to jump start your thinking.

CEO of YOU

Example 1:

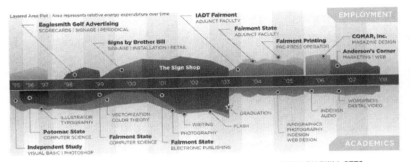

Michael Anderson
RÉSUMÉ / INFOGRAPHICS

theportfolio.ofmichaelanderson.com
lunyboy@yahoo.com | 304-382-5145
HC 63 BOX 2340 | ROMNEY, WV 26757

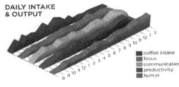

DAILY INTAKE & OUTPUT

- coffee intake
- focus
- communication
- productivity
- humor

PRIMARY SKILL SETS

a. Digital Photography, *Photoshop*
b. Layout, *InDesign*, Typography
c. *Illustrator*, Vectorization, Signs
d. *Flash*, Animation, Scripting
e. Web Design, Wordpress, CSS
f. Copywriting, Editing, Research

Pie slice x represents % personal time investment.
Height indicates approx. professional deployment.

Example 2:

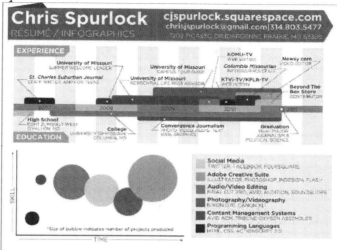

CEO of YOU

Example 3:

Example 4

CEO of YOU

Example 5:

nicole beletsis

3644 Oxford Ct.
Erlanger, KY 41018

p: 859 322 2802
e: nicole.beletsis@gmail.com
w: thesemicolon.blogspot.com

DECLARATION OF SELF:

Diligent, creative, goal-oriented professional seeking gainful employment in a relevant career field. Experience in fast-paced, high-tech settings ripe with intensive teamwork, multi-tasking and customer interaction. Has been involved in all aspects of successful University student advocate organization from daily operations to brand development and public relations. Strengths lie in leadership, strong communication skills, an understanding of objectives as challenges and an unwavering drive to achieve success.

RECENT EMPLOYMENT HISTORY:

UNIVERSITY OF KENTUCKY 05.10 – PRESENT
Student Affairs Officer Temp 1

Responsible for all media materials both print and visual for University Student Center programming. Led branding and design initiatives and responsible for weekly media campaigns. Oversaw staff of 14 and increased event attendance + 16% during tenure. Co-curated programs, events and 'edutainment' services for University students, staff and faculty.

UNIVERSITY OF KENTUCKY 10.09 - 05.10
Creative Director/Visual Designer

Responsible for all media materials both print and visual for University Film Series program. Led branding and design initiatives and responsible for weekly media campaigns. Oversaw staff of four and increased event attendance + 62% during tenure. Co-curated film programming.

OHIO STATE FAIR 07.09 – 08.09
Event Production/Field Officer

Engaged, interacted with and responded to consumer questions. Maintained marketing and information kiosks throughout the fair's duration. Responsible for data collection and analysis.

MERIDIAN CHILES 12.09 – 04.09
Internship

Collaborated with staff on brand redesign and in a media rich environment. Duties included logo concepts, video production and marketing/idea development from boardroom to public release.

SKILLS:

Adobe Photoshop
Adobe Illustrator
Adobe InDesign
Dreamweaver
Fireworks
Basic HTML and CSS
Video Production
Microsoft Word
Microsoft Powerpoint
Microsoft Excel
Copy Writing
Print Making
Etching & Drawing
Basic German
Layout
Typography
Photo Retouching
Enthusiasm
Good Intentions

EDUCATION:

University of Kentucky 08.06 – 05.10
B.A. In Integrated Strategic Communications
Minors in English, Art Studio and Philosophy
GPA: 3.7
Graduated Magna Cum Laude
Deans List 2006-2010

AWARDS:

Loyal E. Horton Dining Award
Lead Designer on award winning program for University Culinary Competition – 2010

Odyssey of the Mind
Co-captain of World Finals bronze winning team – 2006

Portfolio and references available by request.

Example 6:

Example 6: Section 2

 WHAT BETHANY SAYS. . . .

SPEAKER
- Thriving in a Tough Economy
- Simple Changes/Big Results
- Building a Personal Brand
- Socal Newworking

WRITER
- Bethany is currently writing her best book ever. Click on books below to link to Amazon, where you can read more.

BLOGGER
- Winning Strategy Blog: www.winningstrategyblog.com

PUBLICATIONS

WHAT COMPANIES SAY . . .

Bethany is a force of energy and ideas. She is the consummate networker and champion for women who want more from their careers, their lives.

John G. Self
Executive Recruiter /Speaker

Bethany has a talent for creating valued relationships with business executives. I highly recommend Bethany for leadership roles, knowing that she will be an asset to any organization fortunate to engage her services.

Scott Smith, FACHE
Chief Sales Officer at API Healthcare

Bethany is a trusted confidant and skilled listener, who has the pulse of the Healthcare industry in her hands. She is able to provide sound guidance far beyond just her company's solution set.

Joey Sudomir
SVP / CIO
Texas Health Partners

Bethany brings an unusual combination of industry knowledge, sales skills, personality, and finesse to challenging healthcare product development issues.

J Robert Barbour
President & CEO at Advomas

In the nearly 10 years I have known Bethany I have relied upon her healthcare knowledge to provide clarity on critical industry drivers.

Jamie Gier
Vice President
Corporate Marketing
Edifecs

Bethany is the "real deal", a complete CEO. She is a creative problem-solver, innovator and manages complex and overlapping priorities with ease. She is technically saavy, sees where a company needs to go and can develop strategy to support that effort.

Pamela Stoyanoff, MBA, CPA
Executive Vice President
Chief Operating Officer
Methodist Health System

Example 6: Section 3

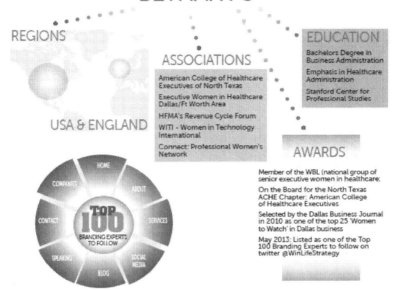

BETHANY'S

REGIONS

USA & ENGLAND

ASSOCIATIONS

American College of Healthcare Executives of North Texas

Executive Women in Healthcare Dallas/Ft Worth Area

HFMA's Revenue Cycle Forum

WITI - Women in Technology International

Connect: Professional Women's Network

EDUCATION

Bachelors Degree in Business Administration

Emphasis in Healthcare Administration

Stanford Center for Professional Studies

AWARDS

Member of the WBL (national group of senior executive women in healthcare:

On the Board for the North Texas ACHE Chapter: American College of Healthcare Executives

Selected by the Dallas Business Journal in 2010 as one of the top 25 'Women to Watch' in Dallas business

May 2013: Listed as one of the Top 100 Branding Experts to follow on twitter @WinLifeStrategy

EXPERIENCE RESULTS.

Contact Bethany to deliver the results you have been looking for.

CEO of YOU

These examples are intended to spark you towards innovative thinking. Hopefully these examples will challenge you to think about taking your resume and marketing efforts up a notch. Are you really packaging up your resume the best way that you can? Have you taken your experience and qualifications and marketed them as solidly and fervently as you market your employer's company? Are you adequately representing YOU?

Some positions are better suited for an info graphic resume. Other positions will never fit into a resume of this type. Consider how you can blow out the seams. Push the limits. Explore options to stand out so far ahead of the crowd that it seems like they are not in the same marathon.

Be unique. You could create a visual info graphic for Page One and a standard Page Two of your resume. How can you change it up? What can you do that will be so far outside of the norm that you will compel them to want to talk to you? What can you do to catapult yourself into the stratosphere? Think astronaut and the Milky Way. Maybe you could create a Prezi resume, or a 'Prezume' as they call it, on the page of their website that lists examples of how to use the Prezi tool. [Prezi is a new presentation tool that is web based. You can find it on the internet at prezi.com.] People have used it to create unique resumes. You could do the same.

Glossi is another example. Create a Glossi online that advertises you.

As Chief Marketing Officer of YOU. your goal is to passionately and insanely package up your skills and experience to ensure that you land at the top of the stack.

You may not be looking for a job. It isn't about you seeking a new position at this moment in time. This is about marketing yourself so well that when you are looking, whenever that is, finding a job will be easy because you will already have jobs waiting in the backlog for you. You will already know about opportunities, and you will already know where to look first. You will have taken calls from recruiters who have called you because of your amazing brand. You will have looked at opportunities and kept an eye on openings.

This is about creating **NIKE**-level value for your skillsets. This is about creating YOU as a known brand. This is about helping YOU to garner the highest possible wage for your distinct skillset. You are working to not just be known as 'one of the rest'; but standing apart from the others to create the highest value proposition possible.

You are preparing the marketing and packaging of YOU to make sure that you are a hot commodity in the market when and if you ever need to find a position today or in the future. You are boosting your worth, building your value and cementing your brand equity.

> ***Key Point:***
> *Have you taken your experience and qualifications and marketed them as solidly and fervently as you market your employer's company?*

Your LinkedIn Profile

Your goal is to create an online billboard at LinkedIn.com that appeals to the potential customers, employers, future equity partners, employees that you may someday hire, or employers that may hire you. This is a source of marketing YOU. This is your billboard. Make it as well thought out as a billboard for Guess Jeans and as attention grabbing as a magazine advertisement for Abercrombie and Fitch. I'm not asking you to put a half-naked picture on your LinkedIn profile, but it should grab someone's attention. Plan it out like you would plan a marketing campaign for a billion dollar company. This is next generation competition. This is taking it up a level. This is putting together a profile that stands apart from all others.

You will aim to create an appealing representation of the work that you have done and continue to do. You will highlight your interests and passions, as well as the reason that someone may want to seek you out to offer you a better position, equity for a company, or hire the services of you provide. Your online billboard should make them want to bookmark your page for future reference.

Your LinkedIN.com profile photo should be great. It should be the one you would use on the back cover of a book you wrote, or to accompany an article you've written, or on a pretend biography you'd send to the President of the United States following a hypothetical dinner invitation. It should not be a photo that you snapped in your office or quickly snapped in your car. This is your professional image. Make it professional. Make it worth posting.

There are other considerations for creating a fabulous LinkedIn profile. Read on for more great positioning ideas.

Step Away from the Title
Within the corporate world, we have become addicted to titles. These titles within our company do not mean much

to people outside of our company. Work on explaining what you do in an industry standard way that appeals to people at any company, not just your company.

If you are working in a big company, there are internal benefits to building a great LinkedIn profile. There could be important leaders within your company that do not know you and do not know what you do. This is not a great position to be in: if a position comes open that's 'perfect' for you, they won't know it.

Write a Fantastic Advertisement

Your LinkedIn profile is really much more than an online resume. It is an advertisement for your services. It should show the Return on Investment that companies have benefited from having YOU on their staff, or the benefits of your company's services. It should be a results-oriented view of YOU. The reader should be excited about what YOU could do for their company.

Surf Around LinkedIn Profiles
What jumps out at you? What amazes you? Your profile should amaze others. It is a competitive landscape. Spend some time on it. Refine it until it jumps off the page. If you are stuck at the starting line on your LinkedIn profile, consider hiring some help. Create a LinkedIn profile that will stand out in a crowded marketplace. Find simple branding packages to purchase online at BrandYOUnow.com.

CEO of YOU

Your Marketing Plan

So, what do you do once you've prepared amazing marketing materials for yourself? You prepare a marketing plan to announce yourself to the marketplace. You promote YOU.

Who will you share information with? In what mediums of communication will you share it? In what time frames will you distribute information to keep your network up to date?

Today I received an email from Nancy Ruff, leader of a consulting practice in Dallas for a Revenue Cycle practice. She was sharing an article she'd written that was recently published. It was a great example of keeping a network member up to date. It was a fabulous example of her personal marketing efforts.

How will you keep your network up-to-date? How often will you summarize information and distribute your messages. Begin a list of communications and time intervals for messages that you'd like to send out to your network to highlight your accomplishments.

Consider sending out these messages at least quarterly. Decide to deliver positive brand messages via a variety of modes that will keep your impressions up and keep your name in the marketplace.

Chapter 6: Work Skills Necessary to Survive in the Future, into 2020 & Beyond

Empathy & Personal Skills

What occupations make up the jobs of tomorrow and what skillsets will you need to flourish for the next ten to twenty years? You'll need to have a plan and be prepared to move in the right direction. As CEO of YOU, like a great city planner, you need a ten-year plan, even if it is only slightly sketched out to watch for future trends and make a rough sketch of what the future might hold.

In our fast-paced, digital world where everyone is spending an immense amount of time with technology, the fastest growing occupations have a common thread: each of the jobs have something to do with empathy.

The U.S. Bureau of Labor Statistics compiled a list of fastest growing occupations in the U.S. by 2020. Each of these occupations is expected to grow by at least twenty percent:

- Sports coaches
- Fitness trainers
- Masseuses
- Registered nurses
- Physical therapists
- School psychologists
- Music tutors

CEO of YOU

- Pre-school teachers
- Speech language pathologists
- Personal financial planners
- Chauffeurs
- Private detectives

Apparently, there is no substitute for the magic of a face-to-face interaction with someone else who cares. Technology may be able to monitor our heart rates and track our blood pressure, but data by itself is useless. It is more valuable in the hands of someone that convinces us to take a new path.

It seems that the more time we spend with machines the greater we cherish a little conversation with wait staff and bartenders who know us. Recently, the U.S. economy added 175,000 jobs in one month. The surprising growth was from restaurants and bars. People are paying extra to talk to other people who can keep the timeless art of conversation alive.

Psychologist, author and Harvard professor Howard Gardner describes attributes critical to success in a 21st Century landscape of accelerating change and information overload in his book *5 Minds for the Future*. Gardner describes five 'thinking' characteristics–disciplined, synthesizing, creating, respectful and ethical–as ways of thinking that will be necessary for tangible success.

But is it that simple? Research is available on work skills that we will need to survive in the future. Let's look at the data available today as we begin to map out your ten-year plan.

Future Works Skills that You Will Need in 2020

The Institute for the Future for Apollo Research Institute, in Palo Alto, Calif., released a study on the future work skills that we will need to survive in the next ten years.

This study doesn't predict what the jobs will exist in the future; it has simply analyzed key drivers that are reshaping the world and the landscape of the way we work. It identifies necessary work skills that you should think about for your future. Start preparing yourself for tomorrow.

So, what are the key skills you will need to survive in 2020? Included here are some examples and ideas found within the Apollo Research Institute's list of skills. Read on for a list of these skill ideas and take note of the skills you may need to develop to be prepared for the future.

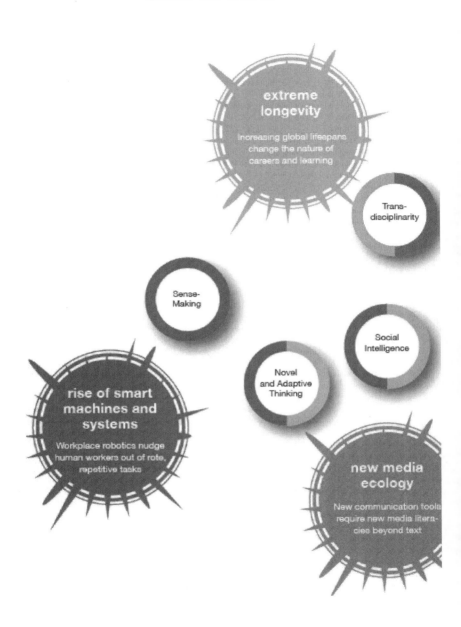

Bethany A. Williams

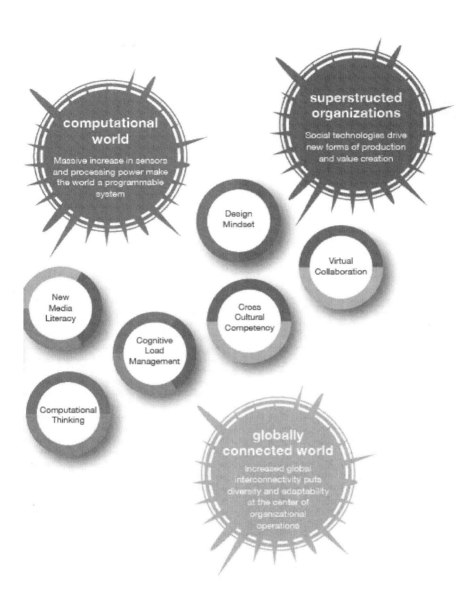

Photo courtesy of The Future Work Skills Report from The Institute for the Future for Apollo Research Institute, in Palo Alto, Calif.

80

CEO of YOU

Sense-Making

Our world is becoming more and more digital. This trend is causing an increasing demand for the skills that computers do not do well, such as higher-level thinking skills. We cannot 'code' these skills. A critical component to success in the future will be skills that help to create unique insights that are important for decision making.

> **Key Point:**
> *It will require critical thinking and unique insights to evaluate the rapid market changes and to assimilate the necessary changes into the company at a pace that the company can both absorb and continue to grow.*

We see this today in the technology and software industries. Although companies in these industries have a whole host of amazing and brilliant engineers at their disposal, they still struggle to figure out which useful technologies will be successful and which will fail.

Critical thinking will be necessary in a growing number of managerial positions, as well as in the social media, advertising, print, learning, and workforce development areas that rapidly change. As healthcare evolves with Obamacare, and rapid changes in reimbursement and healthcare delivery, unique and different approaches to healthcare delivery will be of critical importance. Healthcare will require a new breed of leaders and decision makers that can make sense of the madness, and can take new technology and trends, know what to deem worthless and what is valuable, and understand how to implement these solutions across varied and complex delivery systems.

Disruption is critical to businesses success today. How will we take the disruptive new inventions and determine how to cannibalize our own market share and businesses to build a better future? New skillsets will be require to take complex value drivers and figure out a way to morph organizations forward, so as not to become obsolete as technology changes. This has been difficult even in slow-moving industries. Think of how Kodak has struggled now that you can no longer buy 110mm film. Or consider the fall from high revenues to dismal futures that the big copier companies have had now that there are cheaper, lighter, better copiers on the market that don't cost hundreds of thousands of dollars.

I remember not so long ago when I sat on a plane and had nothing to do but read a paperback, a newspaper, or work on my computer. Now passengers have portable tablets that allow them to watch movies, read books, and play an assortment of games. Internet availability on planes allows real-time access to email, social media, and online services.

The speed of inventions is outpacing our ability to react to the changes. Like watching a rocket ship fly past us, these inventions are speeding us into a future that is changing before our eyes and companies are ill prepared to keep their workforce educated and prepared to work in the midst of such great change.

Social Intelligence

There has always been a key skill that we need to collaborate and build relationships of trust, but now it is even more important as we need to collaborate with larger groups of people not only at one organization in one location, but more likely at numerous organizations around the globe.

> **Key Point:**
> *New survival requires collaboration. Our market is now too competitive, and moving too quickly to not take everyone's opinion, even the youngest one at the table, into account as you look at strategies and issues facing your organization.*

You will need to develop the ability to connect to others in a deep and meaningful way, to sense and stimulate reactions and produce desired interactions and outcomes.

Can you draw the best out of each participant at the table? Can you read their thinking and make sure that their input is received and considered? As the equations get more difficult, it will be become increasingly important to hear everyone out, assess all thoughts at the table, and be sure to adequately assess and consider every idea as it comes to bear. The old days of hearing only the top two leaders and taking their advice are gone. Our market is too competitive, and moving too quickly to not take everyone's opinion, even the youngest one at the table should be listened to.

This skillset will require an eye toward diversity and global social awareness.

The people in this category will develop an ability to be facilitators. They will be able to pull large groups together and facilitate discussions that bring the best out of the whole group. Being aware of their surroundings and information in the surrounding environment, they will know what to ask and how to move the conversation forward. They will become adept at moving the ball. They will learn when to expose a point and when to keep it buried until the organization is able to handle the information and take action on it.

They will be able to assimilate large groups and bring together the ideas and formulate them into a single voice that represents the ideas of the whole. They will be the team leaders that coordinate and assimilate information from their teams.

Novel & Adaptive Thinking

The Institute for the Future refers to "situational adaptability," or the ability to respond to unique unexpected circumstances of the moment. Do you agree? As automation and offshoring continue, there arises a new set of ingredients necessary to survive in the next decade: new thinking and adaptability. With the continual evolution of technology at a quickened pace, leaders of the future will need to adapt quickly and formulate plans to move their companies accordingly.

Large companies struggle to A.) find these skills inherent in their employees, and B.) allow them to thrive in the instances that they do exist. Novel and adaptive thinking doesn't fit squarely into companies that have done the same thing for years. Imagine the forces it would take to change the infrastructure of a multi-billion dollar corporation. Even smaller companies in the twenty to one hundred million dollars a year in revenue range struggle with this type of change.

Employees will need to be able to adapt to an ever-changing environment as well as come up with novel and innovative approaches to 'new thinking' and new ways to do the work. In your mind, envision Six Sigma on steroids. Think about a lean process of thinking involved around consistently rethinking and re-engaging ideas in a new way.

Do you have the skills necessary? New educational opportunities will allow you to easily develop these skills if you want to possess them. I recently signed up to take a few online courses from the Stanford Center for Professional Development (scpd.stanford.edu). I am currently working through the Stanford Innovation and Entrepreneur Courses. Its nine courses cover:

- Empathize and Prototype: A Hands on Dive into the Key Tools of Design Thinking
- The Power of Stories to Fuel Innovation
- Leading Innovation
- Scaling Excellence through Innovation
- Creating Demand: Driving Growth Using Traditional, Social and Viral Marketing
- Building Business Models
- Marketing Innovation
- Financing Innovation: Valuing Projects and Firms
- Cultivating the Entrepreneurial Mindset

There are numerous options that you can find. I encourage you to start gathering information about how to learn adaptive thinking. Consider taking online courses or courses at your local college to infuse new thinking, new concepts, and a new way of doing things.

Krzsztof Gajos, a professor at Harvard, has developed a test to see how well employees can read emotions of others just by looking at their eyes. The ability to read the emotions of others is linked to "social intelligence" which, in turn, is linked to performance on team-based problem-solving tasks. Try it by going online to the quiz at http://kgajos.eecs.harvard.edu/mite/, and see how you do.

We will not succeed in the next ten years doing things the way that we do them today. We will need to be adaptive and novel in our thinking. How will you go about gathering this new skill? Start by thinking about a plan for continual learning through classes, courses and seminars.

> **Key Point:**
> *As automation and offshoring continue, there arises a new set of ingredients necessary to survive in the next decade; new thinking and adaptability.*

We will not succeed in the next 10 years doing things the way that we do them today. We will need to be adaptive and novel in our thinking. How will you go about gathering this new skill? Start by thinking about a plan for continual learning through classes, courses and seminars.

Cross-cultural Competency

In this new global world that we find ourselves in, connected to a global workforce that is cross-cultural and diverse, we need the ability to operate in different cultural settings.

Diversity has proven to be an important cornerstone of innovation. Scott E. Page, professor and director of the Center of the Study of Complex Systems at the University of Michigan has demonstrated that groups displaying a range of perspectives and skill levels outperform like-minded experts. He concludes that "progress depends as much on our collective differences as it does on our individual IQ scores."

Diversity, which is today a conversation companies are dabbling in, will become a core competency for organizations within the next ten years. Success and necessity to outperform their competitors will demand it. Diverse workforces and employees with cross-cultural competencies will outperform those organizations with no diversity competency.

> **Key Point:**
> *Scott E. Page, professor and director of the Center of the Study of complex Systems at the University of Michigan concludes that our company "progress depends as much on our collective differences as it does on our individual IQ scores."*

Scott has documented his discoveries of how the power of diversity creates better groups, firms, schools, and societies in his book, _The Difference_. Successful employees that learn to operate on diverse teams will be able to identify and communicate points of connection that rise above their difference and allow them to build relationships and learn to work together effectively.

Employees with this skillset will identify shared goals, priorities, and values that are consistent across their peer groups and learn to operate together to form innovative solutions that represent the whole group. These combined solutions that represent the whole group will prove to create a higher bottom line for organizations. Cross-cultural and diverse teams create innovation and disruptive solutions that win.

Computational Thinking

I work in technology. It is evident in the area that I work that new skills will be required over the next ten years in the area of big data and computational thinking. The technology sector is not the only sector that will be impacted by big data and computational thinking. As more data enters into each and every component of business, computational thinking will be necessary in a myriad of varied industries and sectors. Will it affect your sector?

This skillset will require the ability to translate vast amounts of data into abstract concepts and to understand data-based reasoning. The amount of data that we have at our disposal is increasing exponentially. New and diverse roles will arise that require computational thinking skills in order to make sense of all the information at our disposal.

Predictive modeling, simulations, and data-driven projections will become core in the decision-making processes. New skills will be necessary in statistical analysis and quantitative reasoning skills. Employees also will have to understand the limits of the data, with complete understandings of the data that feeds the models, and develop capabilities to act in the absence of data.

CEO of YOU

The eruptions of data will affect every aspect of our workplaces and economy. Target has proved that they can tell from buying decisions if there is a pregnant woman in the house even before she makes her first doctor's appointment.

MIT has development an interactive learning environment to teach kindergarteners the fundamentals of computational methodology in a fun, low-risk environment. It is called 'Scratch.' Scratch is teaching kids how to code before they can even read. This ability to think 'computationally' will drive new work environments and new thinking into our workforces and the solutions that we deliver to the market.

CNN Money says that big data could generate millions of new jobs. "US companies will need 1.9 million more techies by 2015." What Top Ten tech skills will these employers seek? Yes, you guessed it, computational thinking. Data analytics is now one of the fastest-growing fields in IT, putting data scientists in high demand.

Peter Sondergaard, a senior vice president at the IT research firm Gartner, predicts that analytics software whizzes will be a scarce, valuable commodity that employers will have to fight to hire and retain.

It isn't just analytics talent on the tech side that will be needed. People that can translate mathematical models into English are also going to be in high demand.

If you are interested in big data, the number one skillset you should begin to develop is experience in Hadoop plus Java. It is the number one necessary skill going forward by a large margin. Dice.com has ranked the Top Ten technical skills big data needs now. We can predict that these will grow exponentially over the next ten years:

1. Hadoop plus Java
   Hadoop powers Yahoo, Amazon, eBay, Google, LinkedIn, Twitter, and many other companies.
2. Developers
3. NoSQL
4. Map Reduce
5. Big Data
6. Pig
7. Linux
8. Python
9. Hive
10. Scala

But the real winner could be the U.S. economy as a whole. Anticipating a multiplier effect like that of the pre-recession auto industry, Peter Sondergaard predicts that "every big data-related role in the U.S. will create employment for three people outside of IT. So over the next three years, a total of 6 million jobs will be generated by the information economy."

Indeed.com agrees that it is a good time to be in big data. They reference what a great time it is to be a data architect, know how to administer a Hadoop cluster, understand the complexities of the R statistical programming language or expertise in NoSQL. They quote an even longer list of skills necessary to manage the growing quantity of data that exists. Employers are looking for employees that know Cassandra, Hbase, and Pig.

CEO of YOU

The job market for people with big data skills is better than ever. These charts paint the picture well.

Hadoop:

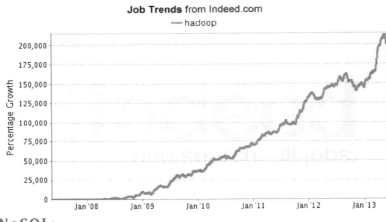

NoSQL:

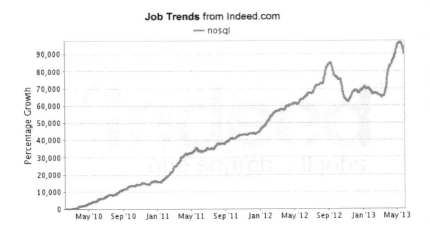

Big Data:

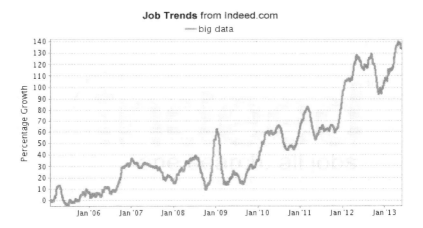

New Media Literacy

New media literacy is the ability to critically assess and develop content that uses new media forms, and to leverage these media for persuasive communications.

This has been more evident than ever over the last few years. Bloggers have begun to be our information sources. Viral YouTube videos have shown us that low dollar marketing can have a multi-million dollar effect in the marketplace for our organizations.

The next generation of employees will need to be fluent in videos and have skills to assess and review videos the same way that they assess papers, advertisements, and presentations today. As the audiences of tomorrow becomes extremely use to visually stimulating presentations of information as the new norm, employees will need more sophisticated skills to be able to use these tools to engage and persuade their audiences that have grown accustomed to visual stimulus and special effects.

This is evidenced by the new focus on inbound marketing and the immense success of Hubspot, emerging software and tools to manage inbound marketing by creating customer inbound requests based on social media presence.

Authors Brian Halligan and Dharmesh Shah created the book *Inbound Marketing, Get Found Using Google, Social Media and Blogs.* Their book covers the new rules of social media. It describes the changing market and discusses pulling your customers in rather than just pushing messages out.

So as people increasingly turn to Google, social media, and blogs to find products and services, the next generation of company leaders will have to know how to take advantage of this change and discover how to use social media tools to be found by customers online.

New skills will be needed to help companies:

- Improve their rankings in Google to get more traffic
- Build and promote blogs, YouTube videos, Tweets on Twitter, e-magazines, and more
- Grow and nurture a community on Facebook, LinkedIn, Twitter, Pinterest, Tumblr, Instagram, etc.
- Measure what matters and do more of what works online

It will be necessary to absorb new knowledge and explore educational options to learn the new media literacy. The Institute for the Future mentions an online class at socialmediaclassroom.com. It includes a repository of resources with lesson plans for learning social/participatory media.

How will we transition into a position where we are comfortable creating and presenting our own visual information? User-friendly production editing tools will make video language concepts, such as frame and depth of field, part of the common vernacular of your future workforce.

Sounds like we have some studying to do.

Understanding Multiple Disciplines

Many of our dilemmas of the future will be too complex to be solved by one specialized discipline. Multifaceted problems will require trans-disciplinary solutions.

It is believed that although the 20th Century encouraged an ever-greater specialization on skills, the *Future Work Skills 2020* report believes that the next century will see trans disciplinary approaches. This has been seen already in the emergence of new areas of studies, such as nanotechnology, which blends molecular biology, biochemistry, protein chemistry, and other specialties.

In healthcare, there is an emergence of a new type of healthcare employee, one that understands a variety of specializations and disciplines. With the increase of big data, combined with the new Obamacare and the HITECH Act, new skills across multiple disciplines will be needed to apply ever-changing healthcare to new and innovative solutions available to solve age-old problems.

The ideal worker in the next decade is "T-shaped," per the Institute for the Future. They bring deep understanding of at least one field, but have the capacity to converse in the language of a broader range of disciplines. This will require a sense of curiosity and a willingness for continual learning even beyond formal education. As people begin to live longer, it allows for exposure to more industries and disciplines. One of the best ways to position yourself for the next ten years is to beef up your "T" skill capabilities. Find an area to increase your depth of knowledge and learn to converse in a variety of other areas as well.

Numerous learning institutions are already positioning themselves to be able to help educate you for the future. As an example, The California Institute for Telecommunications and Information Technology and the University of California's San Diego campus are bringing together researchers from Science, Technology, Engineering, and Math fields with art, design, and a myriad of other disciplines to tackle large scale societal problems.

Design Mindset

As all else changes around us, so will the work settings that we find ourselves in. Companies will begin to learn how to plan your environments so that they are conducive to the outcomes that they'd like to achieve. Even changing ceiling height will encourage open, expansive thinking.

Workers of the future will recognize the kind of thinking that different tasks will require and make adjustments to the environment that will enhance their ability to accomplish these tasks. Think ambiance. New work environments will create work areas that help employees accomplish more.

We see evidence of this already in innovative new work environments. Like Google. Googlers solve complex problems every day in the name of their core mission to organize the world's information and make it universally accessible to their users. They've created cool workplaces that are attractive for employees and encourage innovative thinking and learning. They offer a variety of 'out of the box' benefits for their employees to include:

- On-site physicians and nurses
- Travel insurance and emergency assistance even for personal travel
- Extra time off for new parents and a little extra spending money
- And much more

Most say that Google is home to one of the most employee-friendly workplaces in the world. Employees can eat lunch at one of the company's free gourmet cafes, visit the onsite hair salon or laundry center, get a massage — and bring their dog to work. Google's dog policy provides employees with a basic set of guidelines including cleaning up after the dog, and being mindful of allergic co-workers.

The workforces of the future will have innovative learning environments that will be designed for the work that needs to be done.

CEO of YOU

Photo source: © Drew Gannon

A software company that is creating hospital software may have offices designed as hospital rooms. Toy marketers will have play rooms to explore the toys in creation. Innovation will rule as workplaces will be designed for the work at hand in a creative and innovative way.

Imagine a workplace designed specifically with the work artifact in mind. Think of a place where software engineers with sound proof cubical includes headsets and full screen display walls creating a relaxing and visually appealing workspace. New work spaces will have collaborative work spaces in cool colors with comfortable furniture that allows employees to gather and discuss plans for architectural projects, interdisciplinary clinical discussions, and theme park morning sessions.

Visualize a whole new design created around the job that must get done. This will be the workplace of the future.

Photo source: © Nathan Kirkman

"For Golin Harris' Chicago headquarters, TPG Architecture designed a series of huddle spaces that allow for group interaction and private discussion -- in plain sight. Evoking a retro rec room, the <u>chat</u> space, where employees and clients can work more unilaterally and with less formality, illustrates how office design is borrowing from the hospitality industry."

A design mindset and approach will be a necessary skill in the future of our workforces. The impact our environment has on our mood directly transfers to mental processing.

As the way we work undergoes these fundamental changes due to globalization and digitalization on the one hand and evolving corporate cultures, collaboration methods, working procedures, and hierarchical structures on the other, a range of new opportunities open up for you to help drive the change. For ideas to begin thinking this way, explore the book *Workscape: New Spaces for New Work* by

CEO of YOU

Borges, Ehmann and Klanten. This book features an outstanding selection of examples from world-famous architects who are implementing projects for large, innovative firms, and pushing architectonic and aesthetic boundaries in the process.

Workers of the future will become adept at creating work environments that enhance our ability to accomplish necessary tasks. Start designing your new office space.

Cognitive Load Management

We are living in information and data overload. This is only going to increase; we see no signs of less information in the future, only more. We are drowning in information. In the next ten years, our employees will need an ability to discriminate and filter information for importance. They will need to understand how to maximize cognitive functioning using a variety of tools and techniques.

They will have to review an excess amount of data and information and be able to assimilate that data, picking out what is important and what is not. Employees will need to able to turn the massive amounts of data into an advantage by effectively filtering and focusing on the most important elements of the data.

We are drowning in information, yet in need of data. *How will our future workforce gather all the information available and distill it down to the smallest, most important, components of information?* They will have to figure out how to do just that.

Employees will have to become adept at utilizing new tools to help them deal with this information overflow. They will develop their own techniques for tackling the problem of excessive data. They will use ranking, tagging and even adding metadata to content to help higher quality and relevant data and information rise above the "noise" of too much data.

Our workforce of 2020 will need to develop an idea of how to define their information requirements, seek out the information and an ability to perform quantitative and qualitative analysis. They will need to enhance their skills to have a capability to change rapidly that is comprised of information as well as process and systems components.

Researchers at Tufts have created adaptive user interfaces (also known as AUI) that can reduce the level of detail in the display of information when sensors detect that the users are experiencing high mental overload. Imagine if your screen changed to a simpler display because you were looking at 2 screens instead of one and it 'knew' that you needed an easier display to be able to easily use the information.

An adaptive user interface is a user interface (UI) which adapts and changes its layout and elements to the needs of the user or context. Krzsztof Gajos, from Harvard, has done extensive work on automatically generating personal user interfaces. In this instance, the role of the designer of the user interfaces changes to someone that sets up the ways in which a computer can decide to create a user interface. The users, on the receiving end, then have a changing user experience based on the activities that they are doing.

Imagine if your screen simplified based on the number of tasks you were working on. Think of new 'tagging' tools that will allow you to identify work items that you want to come back to later. New tools are being developed that will help us all to manage the mountains of information before us with ease.

Virtual Collaboration

We've reach one of my favorite skills that we will see increase exponentially in the next ten years: the ability to work productively, drive engagements, and demonstrate presence as a member of a virtual team. I have been working virtually for more than 20 years. I think, dream, sleep, work, collaborate, live, and love virtual teams.

The GE team that I managed consisted of people that had offices in various cities around the world. Each checked into a virtual 'office' by activating their Instant Messenger. We could see who was available and who could take calls and answer quick questions. Messages next to employee names let us know who was on vacation, and who was in their 'virtual' office. We had an easy view of the team and were able to collaborate across a team that covered over seven states, two countries, and even included one employee that lived on an island in Alaska.

Today, as a remote employee, I stay connected through connective technologies. I use Skype to attend Operating Council Meetings and am able to use an Iphone application called Facetime to connect with a group of people sitting in the corporate offices in other cities. In my place at the board room table during these meetings, occasionally sits an Ipad with a Skype session running. On my end, I use an iPhone to display the faces of those at the table. I access all other services on the corporate system through a Virtual Private Network.

CEO of YOU

As a leader of a virtual team, individuals will need to develop strategies for engaging and motivating dispersed groups. The *Future Work Skills 2020* report comments on the techniques borrowed from the gaming industry which are expected to work effectively in engaging large virtual communities.

Collaborative platforms that include gaming features such as immediate feedback, clear objectives, and a staged series of challenges will significantly drive participation and motivation. Can you envision how much the world of work is changing? How will all of this affect you?

We already see that some work teams today use Yammer within the corporations to facilitate an easy flow of information amongst remote employees across varying locations. Yammer is a Twitter-like micro blogging service focused on business. Individuals can only access it if their email address can assess the company network.

Next generation employees will work on their computer, while using Facetime or Skype to contact a co-worker in another office on their mobile device.

New water coolers allow a break room in one location to connect to break rooms in other locations, allowing the 'break participants' to chat, catch up, and have general non-work related/casual conversations for relationship building. Can you visualize this change in your workplace? Consider becoming a proponent to test this at your office.

These tools will help to create a sense of camaraderie and enable employees to bond together.

Companies will figure out high-definition presentation capabilities that will allow senior leadership teams and sales leadership to give presentations and collaborate with prospective customers without ever leaving their office.

New tools have already emerged to help manage virtual teams. Google docs are used in some workforces today to handle collaborative documents. The Microsoft Office Suite has a Lync network for instant communication. More and more tools are being developed to handle the increasing need to manage across geographic locations for remote workforces.

Socialtext is another example of such a tool. Labeled social software, Socialtext is a combined collaboration tool, activity stream filter, and micro blogging/social networking platform. Knowledge is shared through Wiki Workspaces and collaborative blogs which create a hub of ideas on important topics.

As tools evolve and technology continues to enhance, virtual work forces will become easier to manage and participate. Take some time to educate yourself on available technologies and invest time in learning new virtual tools as you discover them. Soon, all of our teams will have virtual members and you will find yourself on a team that spans the globe; so, preparing for it only makes sense.

The Future Holds More Women in Leadership Positions

The most successful organizations in the next ten years will be those that focus on diversity in senior leadership positions. The vast changes in technology and new inventions will necessitate a new and different approach to the workforce. Success going forward translates into more women in leadership. Women in top management positions improve organizational performance when the company is focused on innovation, per an extensive study done of the results of women in top leadership positions by the *Strategic Management Journal*.[5]

In another source, the article "Why Men Need Women" from the *The New York Times* Sunday Review[6], they describe not only the financial benefits to organizations, but also the whole host of indirect benefits companies receive as well.

> "We recognize the direct advantages that women as leaders bring to the table, which often include diverse perspectives, collaborative styles, dedication to mentoring and keen understanding of female employees and customers. **But we've largely**

overlooked the beneficial effects that women have on the men around them. Is it possible that when women join top management teams, they encourage male colleagues to treat employees more generously and to share knowledge more freely? Increases in motivation, cooperation, and innovation in companies may be fueled not only by the direct actions of female leaders, but also by their influence on male leaders."

The Catalyst Organization, an organization focused on raising awareness of how diversity benefits global businesses, has consistently published pioneering research, tools and services that reflect the positive bottom lines that companies experience when employing diverse workforces. They can be found online at catalyst.org.

The Catalyst Organization knows that in order to maximize the benefits of a vast array of talents, backgrounds, work styles, and interests, companies will need proactive supports that embed inclusion into talent management systems, work designs, and measures of team effectiveness, and reinforce it as an essential management behavior. Their paper, titled "Why Diversity Matters," can be easily downloaded from their website.

The Catalyst research found that companies with the highest representation of women in senior leadership had better financial performance than companies with the lowest representation of women. What amount of difference you may ask? They experienced up to thirty-five percent higher return on equity. That is a considerable difference.

CEO of YOU

In Sheryl Sandberg's book, *Lean In*, she discusses what it takes to allow women's voices to be heard in organizations. Women are less likely to raise their hand, represent their input, and stand up and be counted. The leaders in the next ten years will figure out how to pull input out of each member of the team, using diverse methods to ensure that everyone feels safe to share and is able to participate and have their ideas heard and used in the forward movement of the company.

New leaders will read diversity inclusion books, starting with *Lean In*, regardless of their color, race, sex, or religion. They will learn to seek out knowledge on diversity and learn about the characteristics of others on their team.

The male leaders will work to understand how women think and act at work. The female leaders will work to understand how men think and act at work. The next ten years will begin to create a set of leaders and employees that are more culturally competent and able to navigate the rough and ever-changing waters of the new diverse workforce. We will begin to recognize differences and accept them as a positive component of work. More women in leadership will build stronger companies with more powerful bottom lines built upon a diversity mix that both challenges and brings a variety of ideas and opinions to the table.

Chapter 7: Your Financial Growth Plan

At this point of the journey through the pages of this book, you have assembled a reasonable understanding of your current skillsets, and begun to make a plan for added features and skills to your inventory. You've thought about the changes on the horizon and work skills that you will need to have as we move into 2020. Now, it is time to think about your financial growth plan. Just like you had to do with your 401K or retirement account, you need to closely manage your income as an asset and plan for its growth.

You will reach plateaus in your career that will require that you specialize in a niche, take courses to get a certification, complete a Bachelor's or Master's degree, or take on a project or internship. Watch for these stopovers in the journey. Look for opportunities to ensure that you are creating a path that will grow your financial earnings and ensure the best career path for YOU.

It's a Chess Game

Managing your earnings potential will entail watching the board. It is like a chess game. You cannot ignore the game and float effortlessly along on your career journey. Without planning and attention, important opportunities will pass you by and earnings potential will fade. You cannot be too sedentary or content, as it will land you in potentially the worst possible position. Always assume that you need an exit plan. Keep your eyes on the horizon and always know where you'd turn if you lost your current job.

I consistently keep my eyes open for opportunities. I begin working on my next chess move two years before I need to use it. I may never need to use it, but I begin mapping out a plan. What would be the worst thing that could happen if you prepared an exit plan, interviewed, got to know another company, and then decided not to take the opportunity? The best thing that happens is that you form relationships. You get to know another company and, if you suddenly find yourself out of a job, you have an easy call that could potentially land you in a new job. Start the process to find your next job BEFORE you need it. Always be looking.

Passive Revenue Stream

Passive revenue streams do not form without thought or planning. You normally do not wake up one morning and discover that you can make money without doing anything. It won't happen without planning, but with planning, you could create a revenue stream that pays off for you over time. We don't innately think this way. But, companies think this way. We, as individuals, don't think of ourselves as a corporation. Start thinking of yourself as a corporation and managing accordingly. YOU own all rights to YOU and everything YOU create. Bonus!

There are numerous ways to create a passive revenue stream. I'll list a few examples to get you to start thinking of options that may fit you:

- o Recording a music DVD
- o Writing a book(s)
- o Creating a handbook that you sell to businesses
- o Creating Instructional videos

- Recorded podcasts
- Trademarks and patents
- Licensing something you've created
- If you own a business- franchising that business
- Selling a business you've created
- Wisely investing money to create income revenue
- Buying rental property
- Creating a software product and selling it
- Earnings from internet advertisements on your website
- Ghost write a book
- Write and sell eBooks, this has gotten easy with Amazon and Kindle
- Write articles for blogs, find listings at bloggerjobs.biz
- Build a successful blog/niche site
- Create an iPhone application
- Write a 'how to' book/workbook
- Create a curriculum for the organizational development department at your work

There are other examples. One example is lending money on a social lending network like LendingClub. LendingClub is a platform where you can lend your money to other people. You're the bank. Each note is only $25, so you can invest $1,000 and lend money to 40 people. There are many grades of loan (from safest to riskiest) and investors earn, on average, between 5.49% and 13.55% annualized returns.

There are many other examples, begin thinking of options, if applied well to your life over a long period could begin to drive a passive revenue stream your way. Look into creating something that has value then think of ways that you can market and sell that valued item without you having to 'make it' over and over again. Try to get a 'thing' to work for you.

Active Revenue Stream

Your active revenue stream is your income. Just as much attention should be applied to ensuring that you're earning as much as you can possibly earn at your day job. Even if you don't have children yet, or a family to support, think about the future. Decide to work to maximize your earning potential at each and every phase of your career journey.

Companies recognize that they want to hire top talent. They love the thrill of the hunt as well as the chase. In a *Forbes* article, titled "No Career Path, No Retention," Sylvia Vorhauser-Smith discusses three questions that must be answered in the affirmative[1]. She is talking to employers, but we as employees can ask the same questions of ourselves:

- o Are there real career opportunities available at this company?
- o Will I be in a positive position to find out about them?
- o And, are there support structures that facilitate internal career moves?

These are great questions to answer as you explore other employment options that may produce a better paycheck or total compensation package.

You are responsible for building a great income stream for

the Enterprise of YOU. You can build this number to be greater by creating passive revenue, as well as keeping an eye on the horizon and at new opportunities to ensure that you are aware of whether or not you are maximizing your active revenue as well.

> *Key Point:*
> *Just as companies try to place products in the best possible stores to create the best revenue, you have to think about placing yourself in the best possible position to both love your job and maximize the benefits and income that you create.*

It is like shopping for a new car. You weigh out the safety, the size, the needs that you have and you choose the best option based on your particular needs and circumstances in life. You need to do the same thing with the positions you accept and the earnings that you make.

Creating a great active revenue stream is part of the responsibility of the Chief Financial Officer and CEO of YOU. Have you mapped out the best career path? Have you looked at the options that can move you up the jungle gym to the best position for you? What would it take to move your career and earnings forward?

Creating a Map

Create a map of options. What possible career paths could you map out that get you to your dream job? Some of the job sites offer career path advice. CareerBuilder offers career path advice and even tests that you can take to determine the best positions for you. Check them out online at careerpath.com. Career Builder advises that anyone that doesn't take time to look at where they are and where they want to go runs the risk of overlooking opportunities. With no map, you are overlooking potential possibilities to catapult your career and earnings forward. No path equates to guaranteed missing opportunities.

So, how do you create a map to get started on taking career development into your own hands?

You start by knowing yourself. In order to figure out the best possible plan and to meet your ultimate goals at the same time, you must know yourself better than anyone else.

Aricia LaFrance, a career consultant and founder of marketyourway.com, says: "It's likely that you have, for example, always loved numbers or maybe you've always enjoyed helping people. Awareness of those threads can create a satisfying career path. Think life-long interests when it comes to career planning and you'll likely be happier in each job along the way."

What drives you? What passions consume you? Become so familiar with your passions and work diligently to determine what drives you. Explore and map out possible career options. Think of lateral moves to other companies that may interest you. Make a 'wish list' of desired destinations.

You are the maker of the map. You are creating possible journey options. Explore all routes that you could possibly take. You are creating your career journey.

Chapter 8: Using Social Media to Grow the YOU Enterprise

Help Opportunities Find Their Way to YOU

In order for you to 'know' what you know about companies and brands, they have repeatedly packaged their positive messages in a variety of formats, places, and modes. They have, in effect, conditioned you to know what they want you to know about their product or service.

What do you want people to know about YOU and the YOU Enterprise? You need a social media plan that espouses to promote you in a numerous ways across a variety of social media outlets. Lucky for you, this doesn't have to happen all at once. You have a lifetime to think about how you can promote YOU to shed the best light on your skillsets and move you forward into roles and companies where you want to work.

There is a great book titled *Inbound Marketing*. It highlights ways to create inbound contacts rather than age-old traditional marketing. The same is true for marketing YOU. Your goal is to be able to easily spread the message of your capabilities so that people find you.

Your aim is to create a situation where opportunities find their way to you. You want enough brand awareness that opportunities that are perfect for you find their way to your doorstep.

CEO of YOU

In order for this to happen, you will need to think through the kinds of 'perfect' opportunities where you'd like to be invited to participate and in potentially being selected. For those opportunities, what messages would attract them to you? It is a bit like fishing, you will choose appropriate bait and hang the lure and let the fish swim to you.

The intent of your social media plan is to cement your brand positioning and bring in opportunities. There are a host of ways you can discover the uses and benefits of LinkedIn, Twitter, Facebook, Pinterest, Instagram, Tumblr, and the array of others that appear on the scene on any given day.

Depending on your goals and aspirations, it may make sense to hire someone to help you on your social media strategy and plan. As manager and CEO of the YOU Enterprise, it is important to decide how to use social media to advance you forward.

If you aren't comfortable using social media or feel stuck in this area, remember that CEOs do not do everything themselves. They decide the best strategy and plan for the company and then hire people to achieve the goals and plans that they lay out.

This book's aim is to get you thinking more like a CEO when it comes to managing your career and your earnings. This is about the plan and the how, not necessarily about the who, as in who will help you to accomplish the plans and goals that you set out to do. Once you decide on a strategy, it is fairly simple to find resources to help you achieve your stated intentions. You will simply hire these components if you so choose.

I certainly never dreamed that I'd have the number of people that I have working for me. I simply slowly determined that I needed help managing Bethany Williams Enterprises and slowly added resources to help me as I recognized needs and my brand grew.

DIY Plan

You can opt for a Do-It-Yourself social media plan. Slowly orient yourself to the tools and best use of those tools. Often where I see people go wrong is that it is evident that they haven't solidified a message and brand that they are reinforcing with social media. All social media tools are simply tools to disseminate the brand and the messaging that you've determined will better your positioning and get you on a path to where you want to take YOU.

So, it isn't about the tool, it is about the end game. It is about your message and plan. It is about where you'd like to land. Each tool offers differing capabilities. Today, when you want to take a trip, you decide between various modes of transportation. Will you drive? Will you fly? How much money do you have to spend and how long do you want it to take you? Each decision you make on the variables then helps you to select the mode of transportation. Based on your social media strategies and places that you'd like to take your career, experts in social media can help you to decide on a path for your journey.

Chapter 9: Selling Yourself

The best CEOs are the ones that can sell themselves and their company. They believe in their skillsets and are passionate about the company they manage.

As CEO of YOU, developing an ability to sell yourself and your capabilities is critical to your success. It is not a nice-to-have ability, it is a must-have ability. Critical is the ability to not only sell yourself, but to do it with skill and finesse. You are responsible for garnering amazing market value for yourself, understanding your unique skills and talents, and translating your usefulness and value into revenue producing opportunities. Your success depends upon your ability to sell yourself. We often fall short in our ability to sell ourselves. We humbly shy away from touting our success and describing the ROI that a company has achieved because of our efforts.

We are great at selling others, often even selling the companies that we work for, but somehow it feels too prideful to sell our own abilities.

You know your capabilities better than anyone with the exception of maybe a prior boss or two. But that doesn't make it any easier. Have you ever paid more for something because the salesman explained its value and the extent of what it could do? Fully understanding the value helped you to understand why you'd invest that much money into acquiring it. The same is true of your value to an organization. If they understand your worth, they will invest more money into acquiring your skillsets.

"But, I hate selling myself!"

If you're thinking that you hate selling yourself, you are not alone. It is a common struggle for many. We don't think of ourselves as a managed asset as described in Chapter 1. We don't always build a valuable brand and fully understand what we are amazing at doing. But once you've done that, you must catapult yourself into developing a comfortable and confident way to sell your capabilities.

There is a reason this chapter is toward the back of the book. The previous skills you've learned build up to this one. You are to develop an elevator pitch for YOU. As you practice this pitch, memorize it and learn to use it to describe what you do for a living.

Your pitch becomes less uncomfortable the more you say it. I work in leadership in the healthcare technology space. There are thousands of people with a similar skillset to mine. I have moved into a distinct niche, in that, I solely work with organizations in strategy as a growth agent to double market share and significantly grow company size. When I introduce myself, I say that I work in strategy for X company, working to create market disruption with a goal of growing market share and doubling the company revenue. Voila, that is my pitch.

As you become familiar with your skillsets and distinct strengths, you will be able to easily sell yourself. Selling yourself isn't a bad thing. Creating increased revenue increases the benefits that you can provide your family. If you have children, it could make the difference in your ability to pay for their college or the down payment on their first house. This isn't just about you. This is about managing the asset that is the YOU Enterprise.

When I was struggling as a single mom, I solely learned how to sell myself because it was the difference between being able to feed my daughter and myself or going without food. Now, years later, selling myself is much different, but still necessary in that it will determine what I can offer my adult children and how long I'll have to work before I retire.

Convince yourself to acquire this skill. Hone it to a science. Become an expert at packaging up your skills and describing what you do well.

"I don't encounter opportunities to sell myself."

If you're thinking, "I don't run into opportunities to sell myself," then this section is for you. Opportunities are not usually found when you are not looking. It's kind of like winning the lottery you didn't win; you can't win unless you play. As the CEO of YOU, it is imperative to take on an active role in identifying a few potential opportunities a year to run after. Yes, I said RUN after them. Some of you get uncomfortable just reading this. Break out of your comfort zone and decide to find a couple opportunities a year to run after.

Think of a few stretch positions that your skillsets lend themselves to. If you were to move up a level, where could you land? My stretch position would be CEO or General Manager of a 20-50M a year company or VP of Product

Strategy and/or Product Marketing for a 100-500M a year company. So, do you think I watch for those positions? I sure do. Am I seeking a new position? No, but it always makes sense to identify a stretch position and keep your eye on the horizon. You do not know what the future holds.

After you've identified a couple positions that would be great next steps for you, then watch for openings in those areas. Take calls from recruiters for those positions. Apply for a couple roles a year that fall into these categories. Begin to think of managing the opportunities that you are exposed to. If your social media 'inbound marketing' is working, these opportunities will find themselves to your doorstep and you will simply have to say 'yes' or 'no' to the opportunities that arise.

Put yourself into the lottery. If you've branded and messaged and sold yourself well, it is possible that you could be considered for one of the positions you've targeted annually. It only takes a plan with defined action steps to get the ball rolling and right into the end zone.

"It Just Doesn't Come Natural"

Selling yourself may not come naturally to you. It may never feel comfortable. Luckily for you, it doesn't matter if you like doing it or not: if you can force yourself to do it, you will make more money and still achieve your desired positions and career growth. In short, you do not have to like it.

You do not have to enjoy selling yourself, or even be good at it, to 'win' big in the money and position arenas. You simply have to do it. You have to be able to do it a little.

That's all. You will be better off financially if you can convince yourself to learn how to sell yourself.

People that meet me think I love selling myself. They'd be wrong. I hate it just like many of you. I do it because I have to. I do it because it is an important ingredient in the positions I've wanted and the money I've been able to make. It has led to my speaking career and paved the road for the books I write. I've achieved more, made more, been able to do more for my family, all because I've been able to conquer this valuable skill. You can do it too.

When it comes right down to it, you probably would rather not work at all, but you do it don't you? You'd probably like to wake up every day with your laundry done and folded, dishes done, and a hot meal delivered to you in bed. Probability has it, at least for most of us, that isn't how we start our days. The point is this: often things are different than we'd like them to be. Bite the bullet and learn to sell yourself. No, it isn't always comfortable, but it doesn't matter. You will become great at it because you have to.

Preparing Your Pitch

Now is the time for action. Write out a short pitch that describes your unique capabilities. It can start with your title and current position.

PITCH

Hello, I'm _____ ,
                name

I work as the _____ ,

              title

for _____ .

          company

We are a _____

             sector/industry

_____ .

             type of company

I _____

             distinct skillset and benefit you provide

_____ .

             impact you make

Great, you are now ready to practice your pitch and use it every-single-time someone asks you what you do! You are well on your way to making 'selling yourself' just a part of what you do on a daily basis. That wasn't so hard, was it?

Chapter 10: The YOU Network

You can achieve more if you can grow a strong and valuable network. Companies think strategically about business alliances and relationships that they need to build and so must you as the CEO of the YOU Enterprise.

It isn't about the volume of connections you have; it is the caliber of your connections.

Step 1: Figure out Your Connection Strategy

The first step is to determine a strategy for your network. Who should you target? Who would it make sense for you to know? Start a list of aspirational contacts. These contacts are contacts that you will seek out with intention. You will attempt to develop an introduction. Think business development. Think growth strategies. Who should you align yourself with? What connections make sense where you want to go?

Think of taking it up a notch. If you were to get the position(s) you'd like to have, who would be in your network? Target contacts that directionally take you places. Don't be shy. Be bold. Think big. Think Microsoft big. Be Apple innovative. Plan Wal-Mart gigantic. Business developers for companies think about big targets to further their companies. We call it elephant hunting. Go elephant hunting for YOU. Think of a list of out-of-this-world amazing connections and work on a plan to get to them. It all starts with a super-amazing list.

Step 2: Tackle the List with Determination

Once you have the list, work on action steps to get acquainted or introduced to some of the people you've identified. Make your steps as bold and decisive as your list. Send letters. Send gifts. I once sent a gift to Oprah's book agent seeking representation. Why not? Put action steps in place to march toward adding these strategic connections to your network.

Tackle this goal with determination. This could be your next job offer, business deal, speaking event, book deal, or whatever goals you are targeting. This could be it!

Use Twitter to follow those contacts you aspire to meet. You will see events that they are attending and posts that they make. You will become familiar with their messaging and understand how they think about discussed topics. Twitter and Facebook pages allow you to see into their lives and interests.

Ready-Set-GO!

Don't wait for permission. Use your skills and finesse to build a network that furthers the YOU Enterprise. Don't let anything stand in your way.

CEO of YOU

Chapter 11: Reaping the Benefits

You may hate managing your finances. I've met people that have never balanced their checkbooks. We like to go with the flow and let things land where they may. Unfortunately, as with our retirement savings and our bank accounts, that plan is not the best plan toward success and financial benefits for your career management. You must pay attention. You must have a plan. You need to think of yourself as an enterprise that needs to be managed and guided down the path to the best end result.

As you learn to manage yourself as an enterprise, learn to make strategic decisions to grow your opportunities, and consider ways to increase both active and passive revenue streams, you will find a path to increased success and satisfaction.

As you closely evaluate future work skills, and determine how you can apply those skills to yourself, you move the ball down the field and add value to your portfolio. You don't have to be a recording artist or an actor/actress to learn to manage your talent and maximize your opportunities.

What do I do Now?

It's all about a mindset of change. As you read the pages of this book, I hope the information transformed your thinking. I hope you've begun to think of yourself as a managed asset and will embark on a journey to grow the YOU Enterprise by using your God-given talents, setting goals, and driving toward the destinations you've set.

127

Visualize a new future, one that has YOU as the CEO of your enterprise. Imagine a future of financial success where you discover your strengths and use them at capacity to build a great life for yourself and your family.

Manage your career and earnings like the best manager you could hire. Think of yourself as the talent agent of YOU. You will drive forward earnestly to find YOU opportunities. Just like an agent, you will recognize the limited time that you have in the workforce and you will press yourself forward with a vengeance and unyielding determination.

Opportunities abound and it's time to put shyness aside and boldly cut a new path for yourself. With a metaphorical machete in hand, you will cut a new path–one that you've not ventured down before.

Start by mapping out the first one or two steps you'd like to take. See index of potential action steps and check off a few that you'd like to begin.

Failure is not an Option

With a focus on the subjects covered in this book, your prospects for positions and your earnings will increase. You will find yourself with more options at your disposal. The toughest part, once you've created options, is to keep yourself from turning every one down because of a fear of failing or a dislike of change.

It is okay to fall down. It is okay to change it up. Benefits are achieved when we take risks. It is okay to try and fail.

CEO of YOU

The only true failures are those opportunities that we turn down because of our fear of failing. Take a risk.
All successful businesses include a certain level of risk taking. They decide how much risk they can live with and then they exercise that level of risk.

Choose a level of risk that you are comfortable with and exercise that level of risk in your own opportunities. Successful people are those that see failure as 'not an option.' They keep getting up and keep going. Nothing should deter you. Successful people don't give up. Take their lead. Drive forward with a dogged determination. Take risk. Assume ultimate success and continue to drive forward.

You've reached the end of the book. Now the true journey begins. It's time to begin running the YOU Enterprise. Best wishes and good luck on the journey.

Congratulations on completing the book, CEO of YOU. Each of you has a story. Your story could encourage someone else. As we hear from your vast experiences and begin to share our stories, we become stronger together.

Soon I will launch a 'My Story' part of my website to allow each of you to share your experiences and encourage one another. We are stronger together, and it is my deepest hope that by connecting and sharing, our experiences will enrich another life.

I'd love to hear from you. Best wishes in an incredible life journey.

Good luck,

Bethany Williams

CEO of YOU

Connect with the Author via

Facebook

Scan

Twitter

Website:	http://www.BethanyAWilliams.com
Blog:	http://www.BethanyWilliams.info
Twitter:	WinLifeStrategy
Facebook:	LivingtheLifeofYourDreams
YouTube:	BethanyA Williams

See Bethany's other Winning Strategies series books:

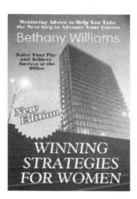

Winning Strategies for Women:

This book provides practical, step-by-step advice for excelling in business, strategies for keeping your job, getting promotions and pay raises, and receiving more recognition in the process.

Learn how to create a situation where YOU become the one working for the greatest companies, achieving the best assignments and receiving the highest pay!

Order it online: http://goo.gl/2f6Xpr

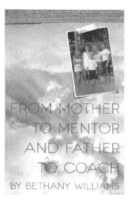

From Mother to Mentor & Father to Coach:

Are fights erupting in your household? Do you have a teenager with raging hormones? This practical guide book will rescue you from the dilemmas that you face with your teenager.

Brimming with tips and insights, it will assist you moving out of the combat zone.   Your role as parent officially changes to helpful mentor and coach.

Order it online: http://goo.gl/QBtk1n

Brand YOU:

Create a Personal Brand for YOU that sells your skills to a market wrought with competition and an ever-decreasing number of available jobs.

In the pages of this book, you will get a boost at creating your own personal brand. You will be inspired and motivated with suggestions and ideas. This book will give what you need to create a list of 'To Dos' to walk you toward increased profitability and success.

Order it online: http://goo.gl/eZ3KFV

CEO of YOU

Live Your Dreams:

Are you living your dreams? Can you accept that you can create a new reality? Make a plan and make it happen. What are you waiting for? Get off the couch of your life and start living the life you were born to live today.

This book was written to motivate you toward living your dream life. It is intended to guide you to the life that you yearn for. It will motivate you into a new day and a new life. It will catapult you into your dream world. Start making a new plan today!

Order it online: http://goo.gl/HjJ9wu

CEO of YOU "To Do" List

Chapter 1: YOU as a Managed Asset

○ Calculate your 'worth'
- ○ Go to Salary.com and/or run internet searches for salary surveys in your field

○ Make a list of potential upgrades
- ○ Education? _____
- ○ Classes? _____
- ○ Webinar Topics? _____
- ○ Certifications/degrees? _____

○ Map out a possible career path

Chapter 2: Personal Brand Equity

○ Evaluate your brand

○ Develop a brand strategy/plan
- ○ How do you want to be known?
- ○ What will you do to stand out?
- ○ How will you market and advertise YOU?

Chapter 3: A Personal Board of Directors for YOU

○ Write down 5 names of people that could be on your personal career advisement board of directors:

1)
2)
3)
4)
5)

○ Call them and ask them to be an advisor to you (see script on page 39)

Chapter 4: Your Annual Report

○ Create an annual report for this year for YOU

Chapter 5: Marketing YOU

○ Google yourself and examine the content that you can find about yourself
   ✓ Categorize what you find from 1-4: _____

○ Put together a simple five point outline of a possible marketing plan for YOU

○ Make a list of items that you have/need and which ones you'd like to improve upon:
   ✓ Bio
   ✓ Amazing Resume
   ✓ Updated fantastic LinkedIn profile

○ Create a new resume/presume, or infographic for YOU

Chapter 6: Work Skills Necessary to Survive in the Future

○ List 2 future work skills that you should consider learning more about and preparing your skills for in the next 5 years.

Chapter 7: Your Financial Growth Plan

○ Write down some ideas you have for a passive revenue stream: _____

○ Do you have a career path mapped out? If not, what are some ideas that you could invoke to begin one?

Chapter 8: Using Social Media to Market Yourself

○ Determine if you need to hire help to get you read to use social media to catapult you forward

○ Should hire permanent help in this area?

Chapter 9: Selling Yourself

○ Prepare your pitch
  ○ Practice it until it flows smoothly off your tongue

Chapter 10: The YOU Network

○ Determine the value of your network and put together a simple plan to improve it if necessary

Chapter 11: Reaping the Benefits

○ Time to put the word 'ACTION' into play here as you map out a course and make it happen

References:

1. Vorhauser-Smith, Sylvia. 2012. "No Career Path, No Retention." *Forbes.*

2. Future Work Skills 2020 Report. Institute for the Future for Apollo Research Institute, Palo Alto, CA.

3. Braccio Hering, Beth. 2011. "How to Create a Career Path." CareerBuilder.com.

4. Kaufman, Kristen. 2013. "Initiate, Invest, and Engage." PlaidforWomen.com.

5. Dezsö, C. L. and Ross, D. G. 2012. Does female representation in top management improve firm performance? A panel data investigation. Strat. Mgmt. J., 33: 1072–1089. doi: 10.1002/smj.1955

6. Grant, Adam. 2013. "Why Men Need Women." *The New York Times Sunday Review.*

7. Bureau of Labor Statistics. 2012. Occupational Outlook Handbook.

8. "100 Best Companies to Work for." *Fortune* 100 Best Companies to Work for, 2012.

9. Fried, Carla. 2011. "College Degree is Better Investment than Stocks, Bonds, or Gold." CBS Money Watch.

10. 11 Pet Friendly Workplaces by Inc. Photo source: © Drew Gannon

11. "What is the Office of the Future?" Entrepeneur.com.
Photo source: © Nathan Kirkman

12. Muller, Randy. 2013. Global Knowledge Special
Report: 15 Top Paying Certifications for 2013.
globalknowledge.com
See appendix for position listing.

CEO of YOU

Appendix:

Listed here are the top 15 Paying Certifications for 2013 from the Global Knowledge Special Report with associated highest earning potential listed in US dollars.

1) PMP: Project Management Professional $105,750
2) CISSP: Certified Information Systems Security Professional $103,299
3) MCSD: Microsoft Certified Solutions Developer $97,849
4) MCDBA: Microsoft Certified Database Administrator $95,950
5) CCDA®: Cisco Certified Design Associate $94,799
6) MCAD: Microsoft Certified Application Developer $93,349
7) VCP-DV: VMware Certified Professional Datacenter Virtualization $92,400
8) CNE: Certified Novell Engineer $91,350
9) ITIL v3 Foundation $90,900
10) CCA: Citrix Certified Administrator- Citrix XenServer 6 $90,850
11) MCITP: Database Administrator $90,200
12) MCTS: SQL Server 2005 $90,100
13) MCT: Microsfot Certified Trainer $89,949
14) CCNP®: Cisco Certified Network Professional $89,749
15) CCA: Citrix Certified Administrator- Citrix XenDesktop 5 $89,499